Microsoft®
Windows® 8

ILLUSTRATED Essentials

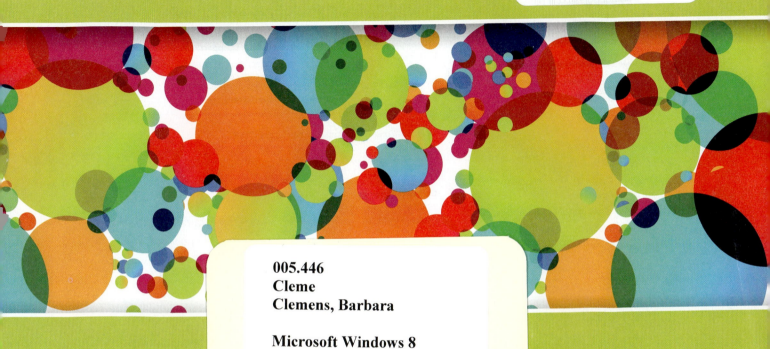

COURSE TECH
CENGAGE Learn

Australia • Brazil • United States

COURSE TECHNOLOGY
CENGAGE Learning·

Microsoft® Windows® 8—Illustrated Essentials
Barbara Clemens

Editor-in-Chief: Marie Lee

Executive Editor: Marjorie Hunt

Associate Acquisitions Editor: Amanda Lyons

Senior Product Manager: Christina Kling-Garrett

Product Manager: Kimberly Klasner

Editorial Assistant: Brandelynn Perry

Director of Marketing: Cheryl Costantini

Brand Manager: Elinor Gregory

Developmental Editor: Mary-Terese Cozzola

Senior Content Project Manager: Catherine G. DiMassa

Copyeditor: Mark Goodin

Proofreader: Kim Kosmatka

Indexer: Alexandra Nickerson

QA Manuscript Reviewers: Serge Palladino, Jeff Schwartz

Cover Designer: GEX Publishing Services

Cover Artist: © Shutterstock/Eliks

Composition: GEX Publishing Services

For product information and technology assistance, contact us at
Cengage Learning Customer & Sales Support, 1-800-354-9706
For permission to use material from this text or product, submit all requests online at **www.cengage.com/permissions**
Further permissions questions can be emailed to
permissionrequest@cengage.com

Library of Congress Control Number: 2012952866

ISBN-13: 978-1-285-17011-4
ISBN-10: 1-285-17011-3

Course Technology
20 Channel Center Street
Boston, MA 02210
USA

Cengage Learning is a leading provider of customized learning solutions with office locations around the globe, including Singapore, the United Kingdom, Australia, Mexico, Brazil, and Japan. Locate your local office at:
international.cengage.com/region

Cengage Learning products are represented in Canada by Nelson Education, Ltd.

To learn more about Course Technology, visit **www.cengage.com/coursetechnology**

To learn more about Cengage Learning, visit **www.cengage.com**

Purchase any of our products at your local college store or at our preferred online store **www.cengagebrain.com**

Printed in the United States of America
1 2 3 4 5 6 7 18 17 16 15 14 13 12

`0 1021 0270413 1`

Contents

Preface

Welcome to *Microsoft Windows 8—Illustrated Essentials*. This book has a unique design: Each skill is presented on two facing pages, with steps on the left and screens on the right. The layout makes it easy to learn a skill without having to read a lot of text and flip pages to see an illustration.

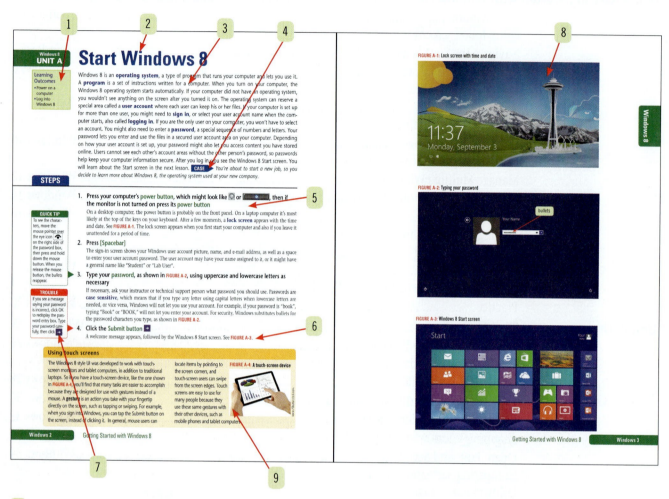

1 New! Learning Outcomes box lists measurable learning goals for which a student is accountable in that lesson.

2 Each two-page spread focuses on a single skill.

3 Introduction briefly explains why the lesson skill is important.

4 A case scenario motivates the steps and puts learning in context.

5 Step-by-step instructions and brief explanations guide students through each hands-on lesson activity.

6 New! Figure references are now in red bold to help students refer back and forth between the steps and screenshots.

7 Tips and troubleshooting advice, right where you need it—next to the step itself.

8 New! Larger screen shots with green callouts now placed on top keep students on track as they complete steps.

9 Clues to Use yellow boxes provide useful information related to the lesson skill.

This book is an ideal learning tool for a wide range of learners—the "rookies" will find the clean design easy to follow and focused with only essential information presented, and the "hotshots" will appreciate being able to move quickly through the lessons to find the information they need without reading a lot of text. The design also makes this book a great reference after the course is over! See the illustration on the left to learn more about the pedagogical and design elements of a typical lesson.

What's New in this Edition

- **Coverage** — This book features step-by-step instructions on essential skills including navigating the Windows 8 Start screen and desktop, using the new Charms bar, starting and working with apps, working in "the cloud" using SkyDrive as an example, and managing files and folders.

- **New! Learning Outcomes** — Each lesson displays a green Learning Outcomes box that lists skills-based or knowledge-based learning goals for which students are accountable. Each Learning Outcome maps to a variety of learning activities and assessments. (See the *New! Learning Outcomes* section on page vi for more information.)

- **New! Updated Design** — This edition features many new design improvements to engage students — including larger lesson screenshots with green callouts placed on top, and a refreshed Unit Opener page.

- **New! Independent Challenge 4: Explore** — This new case-based assessment activity allows students to explore new skills and use creativity to solve a problem or create a project.

Assignments

This book includes a wide variety of high-quality assignments you can use for practice and assessment. Assignments include:

- **Concepts Review** — multiple choice, matching, and screen identification questions.

- **Skills Review** — step-by-step, hands-on review of every skill covered in the unit.

- **Independent Challenges 1-3** — case projects requiring critical thinking and application of the unit skills. The Independent Challenges increase in difficulty. The first one in each unit provides the most hand-holding; the subsequent ones provide less guidance and require more critical thinking and independent problem solving.

- **Independent Challenge 4: Explore** — case projects that let students explore new skills that are related to the core skills covered in the unit and are often more open ended, allowing students to use creativity to complete the assignment.

- **Visual Workshop** — Critical thinking exercises that require students to create a project by looking at a completed solution; they must apply the skills they've learned in the unit and use critical thinking skills to create the project from scratch.

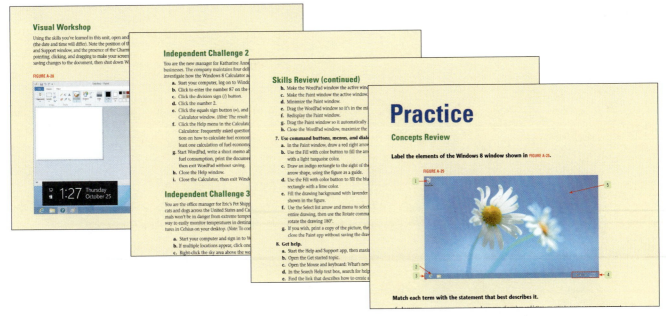

New! Learning Outcomes

Every 2-page lesson in this book now contains a green **Learning Outcomes box** that states the learning goals for that lesson.

• **What is a learning outcome?** A learning outcome states what a student is expected to know or be able to do after completing a lesson. Each learning outcome is skill-based or knowledge-based and is *measurable*. Learning outcomes map to learning activities and assessments.

• **How do students benefit from learning outcomes?** Learning outcomes tell students exactly what skills and knowledge they are *accountable* for learning in that lesson. This helps students study more efficiently and effectively and makes them more active learners.

• **How do instructors benefit from learning outcomes?** Learning outcomes provide clear, measurable, skills-based learning goals that map to various high-quality learning activities and assessments. A **Learning Outcomes Map**, available for each unit in this book, maps every learning outcome to the learning activities and assessments shown below.

Learning Outcomes Map to These Learning Activities and Assessments:

1. **Book lessons:** Step-by-step tutorial on one skill presented in a two-page learning format.
2. **End-of-Unit Exercises: Concepts Review** (screen identification, matching, multiple choice); **Skills Review** (hands-on review of each lesson); **Independent Challenges** (hands-on, case-based review of specific skills); **Visual Workshop** (activity that requires student to build a project by looking at a picture of the final solution).
3. **Exam View Test Banks:** Objective-based questions you can use for online or paper testing.
4. **SAM Assessment:** Performance-based assessment in a simulated environment.
5. **Extra Independent Challenges:** Extra case-based exercises available in the Instructor Resources that cover various skills.

Learning Outcomes Map

A **Learning Outcomes Map**, contained in the Instructor Resources, provides a listing of learning activities and assessments for each learning outcome in the book.

Instructor Resources

This book comes with a wide array of high-quality, technology-based teaching tools to help you teach and to help students learn. All these resources are available at *www.cengage.com/coursetechnology*. The resources available with this book are listed below.

- **New! Learning Outcomes Map** — A detailed grid for each unit (in Excel format) shows the learning activities and assessments that map to each learning outcome in that unit.

- **Instructor's Manual** — Available as an electronic file, the Instructor's Manual includes lecture notes with teaching tips for each unit.

- **Sample Syllabus** — Prepare and customize your course easily using this sample course outline.

- **PowerPoint Presentations** — Each unit has a corresponding PowerPoint presentation covering the skills and topics in that unit that you can use in lectures, distribute to your students, or customize to suit your course.

- **Figure Files** — The figures in the text are provided on the Instructor Resources CD to help you illustrate key topics or concepts. You can use these to create your own slide shows or learning tools.

- **Solution Files** — Solution Files are files that contain the finished project that students create or modify in the lessons or end-of-unit material.

- **Solutions document** — This document outlines the solutions for the end-of-unit Concepts Review, Skills Review, and Independent Challenges. An Annotated Solution File and Grading Rubric accompany each file and can be used together for efficient grading.

- **ExamView Test Banks** — ExamView is a powerful testing software package that allows you to create and administer printed, computer (LAN-based), and Internet exams. Our ExamView test banks include questions that correspond to the skills and concepts covered in this text, enabling students to generate detailed study guides that include page references for further review. The computer-based and Internet testing components allow students to take exams at their computers, and also save you time by grading each exam automatically.

Key Facts About Using This Book

Requirements: You need a computer that runs the Windows 8 operating system. Also, in Unit B, the lesson steps instruct students to save their files to a USB Flash drive. If students don't have a USB Flash drive, they can save Unit B files and folders to a location on a hard disk drive (C:), such as the My Documents folder or a network drive or a location specified by the instructor.

Screen Resolution: This book was written and tested on computers with monitors set at a resolution of 1366 x 768. If your screen shows more or less information than the figures in this book, your monitor is probably set at a higher or lower resolution. If you don't see something on your screen, you might have to scroll to see the object identified in the figure.

Tell Us What You Think!

We want to hear from you! Please email your questions, comments, and suggestions to the Illustrated Series team at: **illustratedseries@cengage.com**

Acknowledgements

Author Acknowledgements

A big thank you to developmental editor MT Cozzola, whose thoughtful and meticulous work made this a better book. Special thanks to the Illustrated editorial and production team who made it all possible, including Marjorie Hunt, Christina Kling-Garrett, Cathie DiMassa, Marisa Taylor, Serge Palladino and Danielle Shaw. And ongoing appreciation to Bill Wiley, who puts up with it all.

Barbara Clemens

Advisory Board Acknowledgements

We thank our Illustrated Series Advisory Board members who gave us their opinions and guided our decisions as we developed this new edition. They are as follows:

Londo Andrews, J. Sargeant Reynolds Community College

Merlin Amirtharaj, Stanly Community College

Rachelle Hall, Glendale Community College

Terri Helfand, Chaffey Community College

Darla Hunt, Kentucky Community and Technical College System

Darenda Kersey, Black River Technical College

Sheryl Lenhart, Terra Community College

Dr. Jose Nieves, Lord Fairfax Community College

Wendy Postles, Wor-Wic Community College

Charmaine Smith, Pitt Community College

Dr. Audrey Styer, Morton Community College

Getting Started with Windows 8

CASE ▶ You are about to start a new job, and your employer has asked you to get familiar with Windows 8 to help boost your productivity. You'll need to start Windows 8 and Windows 8 apps, work with on-screen windows and commands, look for help, and exit Windows.

Unit Objectives

After completing this unit, you will be able to:

- Start Windows 8
- Navigate the Start screen and desktop
- Point, click, and drag
- Start an app
- Work with a window

- Manage multiple windows
- Use command buttons, menus, and dialog boxes
- Get help
- Exit Windows 8

Files You Will Need

No files needed.

Start Windows 8

Windows 8 is an **operating system**, a type of program that runs your computer and lets you use it. A **program** is a set of instructions written for a computer. When you turn on your computer, the Windows 8 operating system starts automatically. If your computer did not have an operating system, you wouldn't see anything on the screen after you turned it on. The operating system can reserve a special area called a **user account** where each user can keep his or her files. If your computer is set up for more than one user, you might need to **sign in**, or select your user account name when the computer starts, also called **logging in**. If you are the only user on your computer, you won't have to select an account. You might also need to enter a **password**, a special sequence of numbers and letters. Your password lets you enter and use the files in a secured user account area on your computer. Depending on how your user account is set up, your password might also let you access content you have stored online. Users cannot see each other's account areas without the other person's password, so passwords help keep your computer information secure. After you log in, you see the Windows 8 Start screen. You will learn about the Start screen in the next lesson. **CASE** *You're about to start a new job, so you decide to learn more about Windows 8, the operating system used at your new company.*

STEPS

1. **Press your computer's power button, which might look like ⬙ or ▭, then if the monitor is not turned on press its power button**

   On a desktop computer, the power button is probably on the front panel. On a laptop computer it's most likely at the top of the keys on your keyboard. After a few moments, a **lock screen** appears with the time and date. See **FIGURE A-1**. The lock screen appears when you first start your computer and also if you leave it unattended for a period of time.

2. **Press [Spacebar]**

   The sign-in screen shows your Windows user account picture, name, and e-mail address, as well as a space to enter your user account password. The user account may have your name assigned to it, or it might have a general name like "Student" or "Lab User".

3. **Type your password, as shown in FIGURE A-2, using uppercase and lowercase letters as necessary**

   If necessary, ask your instructor or technical support person what password you should use. Passwords are **case sensitive**, which means that if you type any letter using capital letters when lowercase letters are needed, or vice versa, Windows will not let you use your account. For example, if your password is "book", typing "Book" or "BOOK," will not let you enter your account. For security, Windows substitutes bullets for the password characters you type.

4. **Click the Submit button ➡**

   A welcome message appears, followed by the Windows 8 Start screen. See **FIGURE A-3**.

Using touch screens

The Windows 8 style UI was developed to work with touch-screen monitors and tablet computers, in addition to traditional laptops. So if you have a touch-screen device, like the one shown in **FIGURE A-4**, you'll find that many tasks are easier to accomplish because they are designed for use with gestures instead of a mouse. A **gesture** is an action you take with your fingertip directly on the screen, such as tapping or swiping. For example, when you sign into Windows, you can tap the Submit button on the screen, instead of clicking it. In general, mouse users can locate items by pointing to the screen corners, and touch-screen users can swipe from the screen edges. Touch screens are easy to use for many people because they use these same gestures with their other devices, such as mobile phones and tablet computers.

FIGURE A-4: A touch-screen device

vovan/Shutterstock.com.

FIGURE A-1: Lock screen with time and date

FIGURE A-2: Typing your password

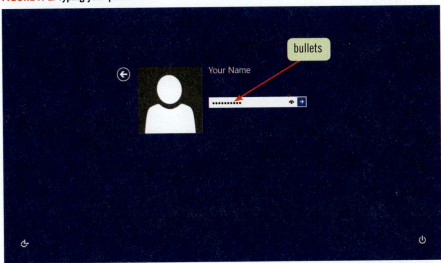

FIGURE A-3: Windows 8 Start screen

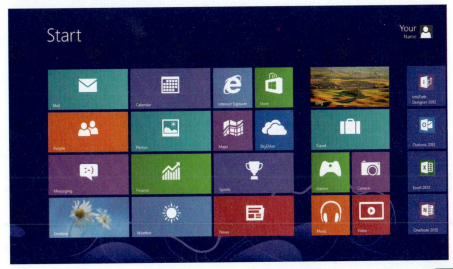

Navigate the Start Screen and Desktop

Learning Outcomes
- Scroll the Start screen
- Display the Charms bar
- Switch between Start screen and desktop

Every time you start Windows 8, the **Start screen** appears, containing controls that let you interact with the Windows 8 operating system. These controls are called its **user interface (UI)**. The Windows 8 user interface is called the **Windows 8 UI**. The Start screen contains many shaded rectangles called **tiles**. Each tile represents an **app**, short for **application program**, which lets you perform a certain type of task. For example, the Photos tile represents the **Photos app**, which lets you view and organize your pictures. Your user name and an optional picture appear in the upper-right corner. You can easily switch between the Start screen and the **Windows desktop**, an electronic work area that lets you organize and manage your information, much like your own physical desktop. **CASE** *To become better acquainted with Windows 8, you decide to explore the Start screen and the desktop.*

STEPS

QUICK TIP

On some computers, you can move the pointer to the right side of the screen to show hidden apps; depending on your mouse, you also may be able to use the scroll wheel.

1. **Move the mouse pointer to the bottom of the screen, then drag the light gray scroll bar to the right**

   If your Start screen contains additional apps that won't fit on the screen, a scroll bar appears when you move the mouse pointer toward the bottom of the screen. See **FIGURE A-5**.

2. **Scroll back to display the left side of the screen**

   The first set of apps reappears. These are **Windows 8 apps**, application programs that have a single purpose, such as Photos, News, or SkyDrive. Some Windows 8 app tiles show updated content using a feature called **live tile**; for example, the Weather app can show the current weather for any city you choose. (Note that the screens in this book do not show live tiles.)

QUICK TIP

You can also open the Charms bar by pointing to the upper-right corner of the screen to display an outline of the bar and then moving down into the bar to display it in full. Touch screen users can sweep inward from the right side of the screen.

3. **Move the mouse pointer to the lower-right corner of the screen, until you see a silhouette of a bar, then slowly move the mouse pointer upward into the bar**

   Pointing to the lower-right corner displays an outline of the Charms bar, and moving up into the outline displays the bar in full. The **Charms bar** is a set of buttons that let you find and send information, change your machine settings, and turn off your computer. When you point to the Charms bar, the time and date appear on the left side of the screen. See **FIGURE A-6**.

4. **Move the mouse pointer over the tile labeled Desktop, then click the left mouse button once**

   The Windows 8 desktop appears. You can use the desktop to manage the files and folders on your computer. A **file** is a collection of stored information, such as a letter, video, or program. A **folder** is a container that helps you organize your files. The desktop is where **desktop apps**, sometimes called **traditional apps**, like the productivity suite Microsoft Office, open in windows. Because desktop apps don't take up the whole screen, you can have several app windows open on the desktop at once, and you can move them around so you can easily go back and forth between them.

5. **If you don't see a blue bar at the bottom of the screen, move the mouse pointer to the bottom of the screen**

   The narrow blue bar, called the **taskbar**, displays icons for apps you use often. See **FIGURE A-7**. By default, the taskbar contains two icons: The [e] icon represents the Internet Explorer application program, and the [📁] icon represents an app called File Explorer you can use to view the contents of your computer.

QUICK TIP

You can quickly move between the Start screen and the desktop screen by pressing [⊞] on your keyboard.

6. **Move the mouse pointer back up over the desktop**

   Your desktop contains one or more small images called **icons** that represent items such as the **Recycle Bin**, an electronic wastepaper basket, on your computer. You can rearrange, add, and delete desktop icons. If you're using a new installation of Windows 8, the desktop might show only a Recycle Bin in the upper-left corner of the screen. If you are using a computer in a school or one that you purchased yourself, you might see other icons, files, and folders.

FIGURE A-5: Scrolling to display apps on the Start screen

Photos app

Bing app

Additional apps

Scroll bar

Charms bar

FIGURE A-6: Displaying the Charms bar

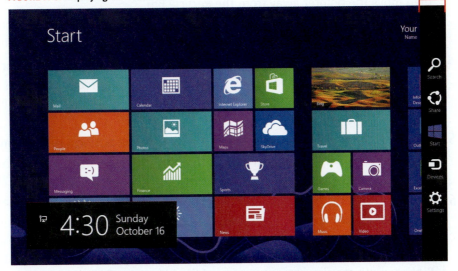

FIGURE A-7: Windows 8 desktop

Recycle Bin

Picture background

Notification area

Taskbar

Getting Started with Windows 8

Point, Click, and Drag

Learning
Outcomes
• Point to, select,
  and deselect
  an item
• Move an item

STEPS

As you learned in the last lesson, you communicate with Windows 8 using a pointing device or, if you have a touch screen, your fingertip. A **pointing device** controls the movement of the **mouse pointer**, a small arrow or other symbol that moves on the screen. Your pointing device could be a mouse, track-ball, touch pad, pointing stick, on-screen touch pointer, graphics tablet, or a touch-enabled mouse or touchpad. **FIGURE A-8** shows some common pointing devices. There are five basic **pointing device actions** you use to communicate with your computer: pointing, clicking, double-clicking, dragging, and right-clicking. **TABLE A-1** describes each action. **CASE** ▸ *You practice the basic pointing device actions.*

QUICK TIP

A pointing device might be attached to your computer with a cable, connect wirelessly, or be built into your computer.

1. **Locate the mouse pointer on the desktop, then move your pointing device left, right, up, and down (or move your finger across a touch pad)**

   The mouse pointer moves in the same direction as your pointing device.

2. **Move your pointing device so the mouse pointer is over the Recycle Bin**

   You are pointing to the Recycle Bin. The pointer shape is the **Select pointer** ⇖ . The Recycle Bin becomes **highlighted**, looking as though it is framed in a box with a lighter color background.

QUICK TIP

The mouse pointer's shape changes depending on both where you point and on the options available to you when you point.

3. **While pointing to the Recycle Bin, press and quickly release the left mouse button once, then move the pointer away from the Recycle Bin**

   You click a desktop icon once to **select** it, which signals that you intend to perform an action. When an icon is selected, its background changes color and maintains the new color even when you point away from it.

4. **Point to (but do not click) the Internet Explorer button [e] on the taskbar**

   The button border appears and an informational message called a **ScreenTip** identifies the program the button represents. ScreenTips are useful because they identify screen items, helping you to learn about the tools available to you.

5. **Move the mouse pointer over the time and date in the notification area on the right side of the taskbar, read the ScreenTip, then click once**

   A pop-up window appears, containing a calendar and a clock displaying the current date and time.

TROUBLE

You need to double-click quickly, with a fast click-click, without moving the mouse. If a window didn't open, try again with a faster click-click.

6. **Place the tip of the mouse pointer over the Recycle Bin, then quickly click twice**

   You **double-clicked** the Recycle Bin. Touch screen users can quickly tap an item twice to double-click it. A window opens, showing the contents of the Recycle Bin, as shown in **FIGURE A-9**. The area at the top of the window is the title bar, which displays the name of the window. The area below the title bar is the **Ribbon**, which contains tabs, commands, and the Address bar. **Tabs** are electronic pages that contain groups of **buttons** you use to interact with an object or a program.

7. **Click any tab**

   The buttons on that tab appear; you can double-click to expand the Ribbon and keep the tab area open. (You'll expand the Ribbon in a later lesson.) Buttons act as commands that perform tasks, and **commands** are instructions to perform tasks. The **Address bar** shows the name and location of the item you have opened. If your Recycle Bin contains any discarded items, they appear in the window.

8. **Point to the Close button [×] on the title bar, read the ScreenTip, then click once**

   Clicking the Close button issues the command to Windows to close the Recycle Bin window.

9. **Point to the Recycle Bin, press and hold down the left mouse button, move the mouse so the object moves right as shown in FIGURE A-10, release the mouse button, then drag the Recycle Bin back to its original location**

   You use dragging to move folders, files, and other objects to new locations.

FIGURE A-8: Pointing devices

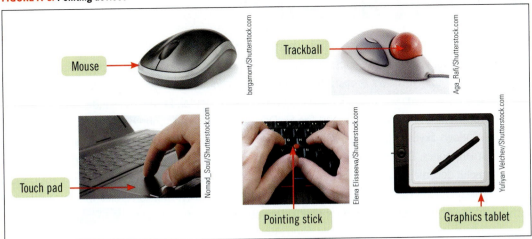

Mouse — bergamont/Shutterstock.com

Trackball — Aga_Rafi/Shutterstock.com

Touch pad — Nomad_Soul/Shutterstock.com

Pointing stick — Elena Elisseeva/Shutterstock.com

Graphics tablet — Yuliyan Velchev/Shutterstock.com

FIGURE A-9: Recycle Bin window

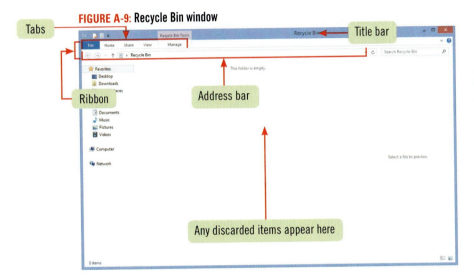

Tabs

Ribbon

Address bar

Title bar

Any discarded items appear here

FIGURE A-10: Dragging the Recycle Bin

Releasing mouse button moves object to this location

TABLE A-1: Basic pointing device actions

action	mouse action	touch pad action	use to
Point	Move pointing device to position tip of pointer over an item	Move your finger over touch pad to position tip of pointer over an item	Highlight items or display small informational boxes called ScreenTips
Click	Quickly press and release left mouse button once	Tap touch pad surface once	Select objects or commands, opening menus or items on the taskbar
Double-click	Quickly press and release left mouse button twice	Tap twice in quick succession on touch pad	Open programs, folders, or files represented by desktop icons
Drag	Point to an object, press and hold down left mouse button, move object to a new location, then release mouse button	Slide finger over touch pad to point to an object, press and hold left touch pad button, drag across touch pad to move object to new location, then release button	Move objects, such as icons on the desktop
Right-click	Point to an object, then press and release right mouse button		Display a shortcut menu containing options specific to the object

Using newer touch devices

Since the arrival of Windows 8, manufacturers have started releasing new products that incorporate touch technology, such as a touch-enabled mouse and an external touch pad that recognizes gestures such as tapping and swiping. So even if your computer does not have a touch screen, you can still use gestures to take advantage of new Windows 8 features using one of these devices.

Start an App

Learning Outcomes
- Start a Windows Accessory program
- Open the full apps listing
- Run an app

The Windows 8 operating system lets you operate your computer and see the files and folders it contains. But to do your work, you use apps. There are three kinds of apps: Windows 8 apps, desktop apps, and Windows accessories. **Windows 8 apps** fill the screen when you open them and are specially designed so they can stay open as you work without slowing down your computer. Examples include the Photos app, which lets you view your photographs, and the SkyDrive app, which lets you connect to files and programs on the Windows SkyDrive Web site. Windows 8 apps also work well on other devices, such as tablet computers or smartphones. **Desktop apps** such as Microsoft Office let you create letters, financial summaries, and other useful documents, as well as view Web pages on the Internet and send and receive e-mail. Still other apps, called Windows accessories, come with Windows 8. See **TABLE A-2** for some examples of Windows accessories. To use an app, you must start (or open) it so you can see and use its tools. **CASE** ▶ *To prepare for your new job, you start a Windows 8 app and an accessory.*

STEPS

1. **Point to the upper-right corner of the screen to display the Charms bar, move the pointer downward, then click Start**
   The Start screen opens.

2. **Point to the Weather app tile, click once, then click Allow if you are asked for permission**
   The Weather app opens to the weather **app window**, showing the weather for a location, as shown in **FIGURE A-11**. Note that Windows 8 apps are updated regularly, so your app screen may differ. To close the app, you will use dragging.

   TROUBLE
   Be sure to drag all the way to the bottom of the screen, or the app will not close.

3. **Move the mouse pointer to the top of the screen, until you see the hand pointer 🖑, then drag to the bottom of the screen to close the app**

4. **Right-click a blank area of the Start screen**
   The App bar appears at the bottom of the screen. Next, you'll open a desktop app called Paint.

   QUICK TIP
   To view all apps on one screen, click the Reduce screen button in the lower-right corner of the screen.

5. **Left-click the All apps button in the App bar**
   A list of the apps on your computer appears, as shown in **FIGURE A-12**. The Windows 8 apps are listed alphabetically on the left side of the screen, and all other applications are grouped on the right side.

6. **Scroll to the right until you can see the group called Windows Accessories**
   If you have a lot of apps, Windows categorizes them alphabetically and groups accessories and application suites.

   TROUBLE
   If your Paint window doesn't look like Figure A-13, point to the lower-right corner of the window until the pointer becomes ⬔, then drag until it matches the figure.

7. **Move the pointer over the Paint accessory, then click once**
   The Paint app window opens on your screen, as shown in **FIGURE A-13**. When Windows opens an application program, it starts it from your computer's hard disk, where it's permanently stored. Then it **loads**, or copies and places, the program in your computer's memory so you can use it.

8. **If your Paint window fills the screen completely, click the Restore Down button 🗗 in the upper-right corner of the window**

Searching for apps and files

If you need to find an app, setting, or file from the Start screen, simply start typing the first few letters of the item you want to find; for example, the letters "P-a-i" for Microsoft Paint. A search box opens, and Windows lists on the left side of the screen all the items that contain the text you typed. Windows lists applications containing your search text, and the Apps category is highlighted below the Search box on the right side of the screen. To see results for a different category, click Settings, Files, or one of the apps in the list, such as Photos, to see matches in that category. For files, you'll also see each file's date, file size, and location. Point to an item in the Results list to see more information, including its location on your computer.

FIGURE A-11: Weather app

FIGURE A-12: Apps list

FIGURE A-13: Paint app window

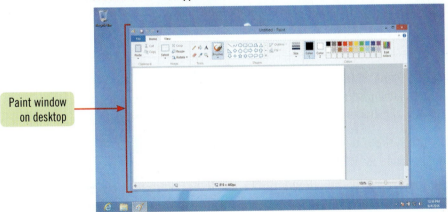

TABLE A-2: Useful Windows 8 accessory programs

accessory name	use to
Notepad	Create text files with basic text formatting
Paint	Create and edit drawings using lines, shapes, and colors
Snipping Tool	Capture an image of any screen area that you can save to use in a document
Sound Recorder	With a computer microphone, make recordings of voice or music
Sticky Notes	Create short text notes that you can use to set reminders or create to-do lists for yourself
Windows Media Player	Play music, videos, recorded TV and show pictures

Work with a Window

When you start a desktop app, its **window**, a frame displaying the app's tools, opens. In many apps, a blank file also opens so you can start creating a new document. For example, in Paint, a drawing app, a blank document opens so you can start drawing right away. All windows in the Windows 8 operating system have similar window elements. Once you can use a window in one app, you will know how to work with windows in many other apps. **CASE** ▶ *To become more familiar with the Windows 8 user interface, you explore elements in the Paint window.*

DETAILS

Many windows have the following common elements. Refer to FIGURE A-14:

- At the top of the window, you see a **title bar**, a colored strip that contains the name of the document and app you opened. This document has not been saved, so it has the temporary name "Untitled" and the app name is "Paint."

- On the right side of the title bar, the **Window control icons** let you control the app window. The **Minimize button** temporarily hides it, making it a button on the taskbar. The app is still running, but its window is hidden until you reopen it. The **Maximize button** enlarges the window to fill the entire screen. If a window is already maximized, the Maximize button changes to the **Restore Down button**, which reduces it to the last nonmaximized size. Clicking the **Close button** closes the app.

- Many windows have a **scroll bar** on the right side and/or the bottom of the window. You click the scroll bar elements to show additional parts of your document. See **TABLE A-3** to learn the parts of a scroll bar.

- Just below the title bar, at the top of the Paint window, is the Ribbon, the strip that contains tabs. The Paint window has three tabs, the File tab, the Home tab, and the View tab. Tabs are divided into **groups** of command buttons. The Home tab has five groups: Clipboard, Image, Tools, Shapes, and Colors. Many apps also include **menus** that display words you click to show lists of commands, as well as **toolbars** containing buttons.

- The **Quick Access toolbar**, in the upper-left corner of the window, lets you quickly perform common actions such as saving a file.

STEPS

1. **Click the Paint window Minimize button**
   The app is minimized to a program button with a gradient shading, indicating the app is still open. See **FIGURE A-15**. Taskbar buttons representing closed programs are not shaded.

2. **Click the taskbar button representing the Paint app**
   The app window reappears.

3. **Drag the gray scroll box down, notice the lower edge of the work area that appears, then click the Up scroll arrow until you see the top edge of the work area**

4. **Point to the View tab with the tip of the mouse pointer, then click the View tab once**
   Clicking the View tab moved it in front of the Home tab. This tab has three groups, Zoom, Show or hide, and Display, containing buttons that let you change your view of the document window to work more easily.

5. **Click the Home tab, then click the Paint window Maximize button**
   The window fills the screen, and the Maximize button becomes the Restore Down button.

6. **Click the window's Restore Down button**
   The Paint window returns to its previous size on the screen.

FIGURE A-14: Typical app window elements

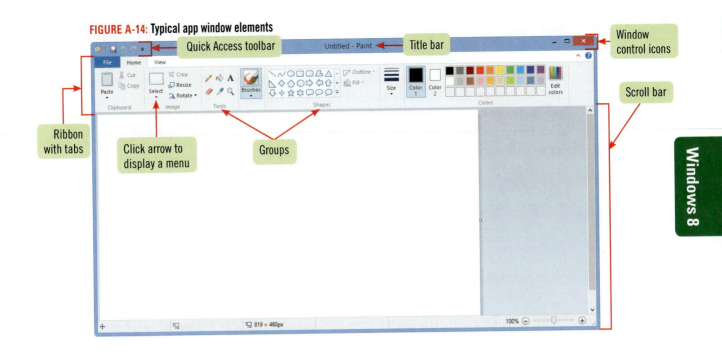

Quick Access toolbar

Title bar

Window control icons

Ribbon with tabs

Click arrow to display a menu

Groups

Scroll bar

FIGURE A-15: Taskbar on the desktop

Icons with solid backgrounds represent programs that are not open

Paint program button with gradient background indicates program is open

Your icons may differ

TABLE A-3: Parts of a scroll bar

name	looks like	use for
Scroll box	(Size may vary)	Drag to scroll quickly through a long document
Scroll arrows	⌃ ⌄	Click to scroll up, down, left, or right in small amounts
Shaded area	(Above, below, and to either side of scroll box)	Click to move up or down by one screen

Using the Quick Access toolbar

On the left side of the title bar, the Quick Access toolbar lets you perform common tasks with just one click. The Save button saves the changes you have made to a document. The Undo button lets you reverse (undo) the last action you performed.

The Redo button reinstates the change you just undid. Use the Customize Quick Access Toolbar button to add other frequently used buttons to the toolbar, move the toolbar below the Ribbon, or hide the Ribbon.

Manage Multiple Windows

You can work with more than one desktop app at a time by switching among open app windows. If you open two or more apps, a window opens for each one. You can work with each open app window, going back and forth between them. The window in front is called the **active window**. Any other open window behind the active window is called an **inactive window**. For ease in working with multiple windows, you can move, arrange, make them smaller or larger, minimize, or restore them so they're not in the way. To resize a window, drag a window's edge, called its **border**. You can also use the taskbar to switch between windows. See **TABLE A-4** for a summary of taskbar actions. **CASE** *Keeping the Paint app open, you open the WordPad app and then work with both app windows.*

STEPS

1. **With the Paint window open, point to the lower-left corner of the screen until the Start thumbnail appears, click the Start thumbnail, then type word**

   The Apps screen appears, displaying apps that have "word" in them, such as WordPad.

2. **Click WordPad, then if the window is maximized, click its Restore Down button in the title bar**

   The WordPad window opens, as shown in **FIGURE A-16**. The WordPad window is in front, indicating that it is the active window. The Paint window is the inactive window. On the taskbar, the gradient backgrounds on the WordPad and Paint app buttons tell you both apps are open.

   > **QUICK TIP**
   > To click an inactive window to make it active, click its title bar, window edge, or a blank area. To move a window, drag its title bar.

3. **Point to a blank part of the WordPad window title bar, then drag the WordPad window down slightly so you can see more of the Paint window**

4. **Click once on the Paint window's title bar**

   The Paint window is now the active window and appears in front of the WordPad window. You can make any window active by clicking it, or by clicking an app's icon in the taskbar.

   > **QUICK TIP**
   > You can also move among open windows by pressing and holding [Alt] and pressing [Tab].

5. **Point to the taskbar, then click the WordPad window button** 🖼️

   The WordPad window becomes active. When you open multiple windows on the desktop, you may need to resize windows so they don't get in the way of other open windows.

   > **TROUBLE**
   > If you don't see the lower-right corner of the window, drag the window up slightly by its title bar.

6. **Point to the lower-right corner of the WordPad window until the pointer becomes ⬂, then drag up and to the left about an inch to make the window smaller**

   You can also point to any edge of a window until you see the ⬌ or ↕ pointer and drag to make it larger or smaller in one direction only.

7. **Point to the WordPad window title bar, drag the window to the left side of the screen until the mouse pointer reaches the screen edge and you see a vertical line down the middle of the screen, then release the mouse button**

   The WordPad window instantly fills the left side of the screen. This is called the **Snap feature**.

8. **Drag the Paint window title bar to the right side of the screen and release the mouse button**

   The Paint window fills the right side of the screen. Snapping makes it easy to view the contents of two windows at the same time. See **FIGURE A-17**.

9. **Click the WordPad window Close button** ❌ **, click Don't Save if prompted to save changes, then click the Maximize button** 🔲 **in the Paint window's title bar**

   The WordPad app closes, so you can no longer use its tools unless you start it again. The Paint app window remains open.

FIGURE A-16: Working with multiple windows

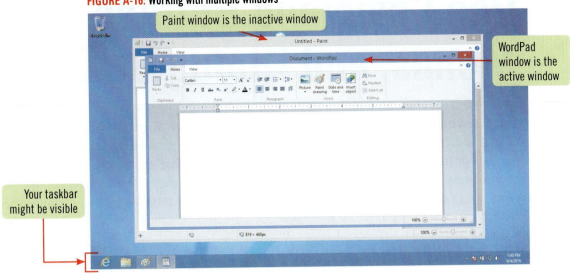

Paint window is the inactive window

WordPad window is the active window

Your taskbar might be visible

FIGURE A-17: WordPad and Paint windows snapped to each side of the screen

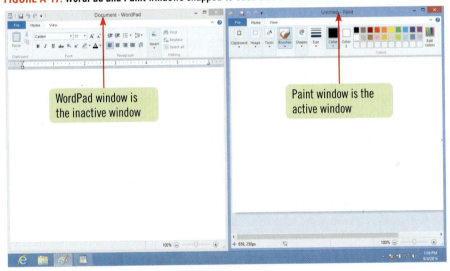

WordPad window is the inactive window

Paint window is the active window

TABLE A-4: Using the Desktop taskbar

to	do this
Add buttons to taskbar	Open an app, right-click its icon on the task bar, then click Pin this program to taskbar
Change order of taskbar buttons	Drag any icon to a new taskbar location
See a list of recent documents opened in a taskbar app	Right-click taskbar app button
Close a document using the taskbar	Point to taskbar button, point to document image, then click its Close button
Minimize all open windows	Click Show desktop button to the right of taskbar date and time
Redisplay all minimized windows	Click Show desktop button to the right of taskbar date and time
See preview of documents in taskbar	Point to taskbar button for open app

Use Command Buttons, Menus, and Dialog Boxes

When you work in an app, you communicate using command buttons, menus, and dialog boxes. **Command buttons** let you issue instructions to modify app objects. Command buttons are often organized on a Ribbon into tabs, and then into groups like those in the Paint window. Some command buttons have text on them, and others show only an icon that represents what they do. Other command buttons reveal **menus**, lists of commands you can choose. And some command buttons open up a **dialog box**, a window with controls that lets you tell Windows what you want. **TABLE A-5** lists the common types of controls you find in dialog boxes. **CASE** *You use command buttons, menus, and dialog boxes to communicate with the Paint app.*

STEPS

1. **In the Shapes group, click the More button** ⬇ **just to the right of the shapes, then click the Five-point star button** ☆

2. **Click the Gold button in the Colors group, move the pointer over the white drawing area, then drag to draw a star similar to the one in FIGURE A-18**
   The white drawing area is called the **canvas.**

3. **In the Shapes group, click the More button** ⬇ **just to the right of the shapes, click the down scroll arrow if necessary, click the Lightning button, click the Indigo color button in the Colors group, then drag a lightning bolt shape near the star, using FIGURE A-18 as a guide**
   Don't be concerned if your object isn't exactly like the one in the figure.

4. **Click the Fill with color button** 🖌 **in the Tools group, click the Light turquoise color button in the Colors group, click inside the star, click the Lime color button, click inside the lightning bolt, then compare your drawing to FIGURE A-18**

5. **Click the Select list arrow in the Image group, then click Select all, as shown in FIGURE A-19**
   The Select all command selects the entire drawing, as indicated by the dotted line surrounding the white drawing area. Other commands on this menu let you select individual elements or change your selection.

6. **Click the Rotate button** 🔄 **in the Image group, then click Rotate 180°**
   You often need to use multiple commands to perform an action—in this case, you used one command to select the item you wanted to work with, and the next command rotated the item.

7. **Click the File tab, then click Print**
   The Print dialog box opens, as shown in **FIGURE A-20**. This dialog box lets you choose a printer, specify which part of your document or drawing you want to print, and choose how many copies you want to print. The **default**, or automatically selected, number of copies is 1, which is what you want.

8. **Click Print, or, if you prefer not to print, click Cancel**
   The drawing prints on your printer. You decide to close the app without saving your drawing.

9. **Click the File tab, click Exit, then click Don't Save**
   You closed the file without saving your changes, then exited the app. Most apps include a command for closing a document without exiting the program. However, Paint allows you to open only one document at a time, so it does not include a Close command.

FIGURE A-18: Star and lightning shapes filled with color

FIGURE A-19: Select menu options

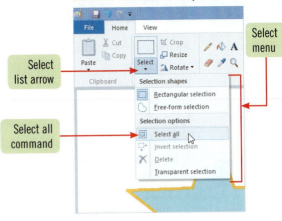

Select list arrow

Select menu

Select all command

FIGURE A-20: Print dialog box

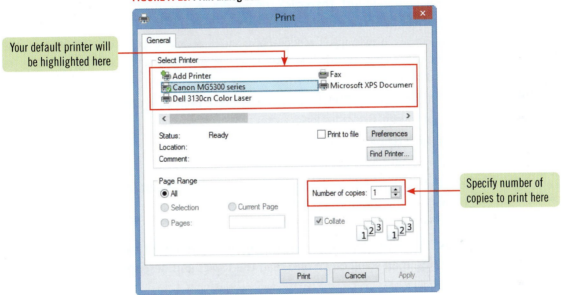

Your default printer will be highlighted here

Specify number of copies to print here

TABLE A-5: Common dialog box controls

element	example	description
Text box	132	A box in which you type text or numbers
Spin box	1	A box with up and down arrows; you can click arrows or type to increase or decrease value
Option button		A small circle you click to select the option; only one in a set can be selected at once
Check box		A small box that turns an option on when checked or off when unchecked; more than one can be selected at once
List box	Select Printer / Add Printer / Dell Laser Printer 3000cn PCL6 / Fax	A box that lets you select from a list of options
Command button	Save	A button you click to issue a command

Get Help

Learning Outcomes
• Open the Help app
• Explore and search for help topics

As you use Windows 8, you might feel ready to learn more about it, or you might have a problem and need some advice. You can open the Windows 8 Help and Support to find the information you need. You can browse Help and Support topics by clicking a category, such as "Get started." Within this category, you see more specific topics. Each topic is represented by blue or purple text called **links** that you can click to learn more. You can also search Help and Support by typing one or more descriptive words called **keywords**, such as "taskbar," to find topics related to your keywords. **CASE** *You use Windows 8 help to learn more about Windows and the WordPad accessory.*

STEPS

1. **Point to the lower-left corner of the screen, click the Start thumbnail once to display the Start screen, then type help**

   The Help and Support app is listed in the found items area.

2. **Click Help and Support, then click the window's Maximize button ▢ if the window does not fill the screen**

   The Windows Help and Support window opens and is maximized, as shown in **FIGURE A-21**. A search box appears near the top of the window. Three topics appear in blue boxes. Below them, you see text briefly describing each topic.

3. **Position the hand pointer 👆 over Get Started, then click once**

   Several categories of Get Started topics appear.

4. **Click Touch: swipe, tap, and beyond**

   Help and Support information appears.

5. **Drag the scroll box down to view text and graphics about touch, then drag the scroll box back to the top of the scroll bar**

   You decide to learn more about the taskbar.

6. **Click in the Search text box near the top of the window, type taskbar, click the Search button 🔍, then scroll down and read the topics and descriptions**

   A list of links related to using the taskbar appears. See **FIGURE A-22**.

7. **Click How to use the taskbar, scroll down if necessary, then click To move the taskbar**

8. **Read the information, clicking any other links that interest you**

9. **When you are finished, click the Close button ✕ in the upper-right corner of the Windows Help and Support window**

   The Windows Help and Support window closes.

Finding other ways to get help

The Windows Help and Support Home window includes a variety of resources for learning more about Windows 8 and solving problems. In the More to Explore section, click the **Windows website** link to locate **blogs** (Web logs, which are personal commentaries), downloads, video tours, and other current Windows 8 resources. You'll also find FAQs (Frequently Asked Questions) about current Windows topics. Click the **Microsoft Community website** (formerly called the **Microsoft Answers website**) link to find **forums**, electronic gathering places where anyone can read and add questions and answers on computer issues.

FIGURE A-21: Windows Help and Support window

FIGURE A-22: Getting help on the term "taskbar"

Using right-clicking

For some actions, you click items using the right mouse button, known as **right-clicking**. You can right-click almost any icon on your desktop to open a shortcut menu. A **shortcut menu** lists common commands for an object, such as emptying the Recycle Bin. The shortcut menu commands depend on the object you right-click. For example, **FIGURE A-23** shows the shortcut menu that appears if you right-click the Recycle Bin. Then you click (with the left mouse button) a shortcut menu command to issue that command.

FIGURE A-23: Shortcut menu

	Open
	Pin to Start
	Empty Recycle Bin
	Create shortcut
	Rename
	Properties

Exit Windows 8

When you finish working on your computer, you should close any open files, exit any open apps, close any open windows, and exit (or **shut down**) Windows 8. TABLE A-6 shows options for ending your Windows 8 sessions. Whichever option you choose, it's important to shut down your computer in an orderly way. If you turn off or unplug the computer while Windows 8 is running, you could lose data or damage Windows 8 and your computer. If you are working in a computer lab, follow your instructor's directions and your lab's policies for ending your Windows 8 session. **CASE** *You have examined the basic ways you can use Windows 8, so you are ready to end your Windows 8 session.*

STEPS

QUICK TIP

Pressing [ ] [C] again hides the Charms bar.

QUICK TIP

If you are using a Windows 8 tablet, press the lock button on your tablet to bring up the lock screen, swipe the lock screen, then click the shutdown button to power off your computer.

1. **Press [ ] [C] to display the Charms bar**

2. **Click Settings, then click Power, as shown in** FIGURE A-24
   The Power button menu lists shut down options.

3. **If you are working in a computer lab, follow the instructions provided by your instructor or technical support person for ending your Windows 8 session; if you are working on your own computer, click Shut down or the option you prefer for ending your Windows 8 session**

4. **After you shut down your computer, you may also need to turn off your monitor and other hardware devices, such as a printer, to conserve energy**

Installing updates when you exit Windows

Sometimes, after you shut down your machine, you might find that your machine does not shut down immediately. Instead, Windows might install software updates. If you see an option on your Power menu that lets you update, you can select it to update your software. A window indicating that updates are being installed, do not unplug or press the power switch to turn off your machine. Let the updates install completely. After the updates are installed, your computer will shut down, as you originally requested.

FIGURE A-24: Shutting down your computer

Shut-down options

Settings

Desktop

Control Panel

Personalization

PC info

Help

Sleep
Shut down
Restart

Network   Unavailable

Notifications   Power   Keyboard

Change PC settings

Power button

TABLE A-6: Power options

option	description
Sleep	Puts computer in a low-power state while keeping any open apps open so you can return immediately to where you left off
Shut down	Closes any open apps and completely turns off the computer
Restart	Closes any open apps, shuts down the computer, then restarts it

Practice

Concepts Review

Label the elements of the Windows 8 window shown in FIGURE A-25.

FIGURE A-25

Match each term with the statement that best describes it.

6. Accessory
7. Keyword
8. Windows 8 UI
9. Active window
10. Password
11. Operating system
12. App

a. A sequence of numbers and letters you enter to access a secure user account
b. The window in front of other windows
c. An application program
d. Name for the Windows 8 user interface
e. An application program that comes with Windows 8
f. Descriptive word you use to search Windows Help and Support
g. A program necessary to run your computer

Select the best answer from the list of choices.

13. You use the Maximize button to:
   a. Scroll down a window.
   b. Restore a window to a previous size.
   c. Temporarily hide a window.
   d. Expand a window to fill the entire screen.
14. Which of the following is not a Windows accessory?
   a. Sticky Notes
   b. Windows 8
   c. Sound Recorder
   d. Paint
15. Which button do you click to reduce an open window to a button on the taskbar?
   a. Close button
   b. Minimize button
   c. Restore Down button
   d. Maximize button

16. **The screen controls that let you interact with an operating system are called its:**
  a. Accessories.
  c. User interface.
  b. Application program.
  d. Taskbar.

17. **Which type of program runs your computer and lets you use it?**
  a. App.
  c. Accessory.
  b. Traditional app.
  d. Operating system.

18. **Which Windows 8 feature lets you find and share information, change your machine settings, and turn off your computer?**
  a. Charms bar.
  c. Application program.
  b. Operating system.
  d. Accessory program.

19. **What part of a window shows the name of an open app?**
  a. Scroll bar.
  c. Quick Access toolbar.
  b. Title bar.
  d. Ribbon.

Skills Review

1. **Start Windows 8.**
  a. If your computer and monitor are not running, press your computer's and (if necessary) your monitor's power buttons.
  b. If necessary, click the user name that represents your user account.
  c. Enter your password, using correct uppercase and lowercase letters.

2. **Navigate the Start screen and desktop.**
  a. Examine the Windows 8 Start screen, scroll to the right so you can display any hidden apps, then display the Charms bar.
  b. Display the Windows 8 desktop, and then display the taskbar.

3. **Point, click, and drag.**
  a. Use pointing and clicking to go to the Start screen, then return to the desktop.
  b. On the Windows 8 desktop, use clicking to select the Recycle Bin.
  c. Use pointing to display the ScreenTip for Internet Explorer in the taskbar, and then display the ScreenTips for any other icons on the taskbar.
  d. Use double-clicking to open the Recycle Bin window, then close it.
  e. Drag the Recycle Bin to the lower-right corner of the screen, then drag it back to the upper-left corner.
  f. Click the Date and Time area to display the calendar and clock, then click it again to close it.

4. **Start an app.**
  a. Return to the Start screen, then use the Apps bar to display all the apps on your computer.
  b. Open the Windows 8 accessory of your choice, then close it. (*Hint:* To close, drag from the top of the window all the way to the bottom.)
  c. Scroll if necessary to display the Windows accessories.
  d. Open the WordPad accessory, then if the window fills the screen, restore it down.

5. **Manage a window.**
  a. Minimize the WordPad window.
  b. Redisplay the window using a taskbar button.
  c. In the WordPad window, click the File tab on the Ribbon, then click the About WordPad command.
  d. Read the contents of the window, then close the About WordPad dialog box by clicking OK.
  e. Maximize the WordPad window, then restore it down.
  f. Display the View tab in the WordPad window.

6. **Manage multiple windows.**
  a. Leaving WordPad open, go to the Start screen and use typing to locate the Paint app, open Paint, then restore down the Paint window if necessary.

Skills Review (continued)

b. Make the WordPad window the active window.

c. Make the Paint window the active window.

d. Minimize the Paint window.

e. Drag the WordPad window so it's in the middle of the screen.

f. Redisplay the Paint window.

g. Drag the Paint window so it automatically fills the right side of the screen.

h. Close the WordPad window, maximize the Paint window, then restore down the Paint window.

7. Use command buttons, menus, and dialog boxes.

a. In the Paint window, draw a red right arrow shape, similar to the one shown in **FIGURE A-26**.

b. Use the Fill with color button to fill the arrow with a light turquoise color.

c. Draw an indigo rectangle to the right of the arrow shape, using the figure as a guide.

d. Use the Fill with color button to fill the blue rectangle with a lime color.

e. Fill the drawing background with lavender as shown in the figure.

f. Use the Select list arrow and menu to select the entire drawing, then use the Rotate command to rotate the drawing 180°.

g. If you wish, print a copy of the picture, then close the Paint app without saving the drawing.

FIGURE A-26

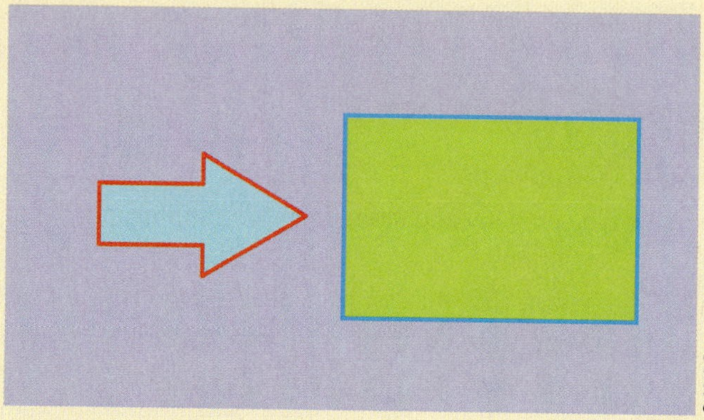

© 2013 Cengage Learning

8. Get help.

a. Start the Help and Support app, then maximize the window if it's not already maximized.

b. Open the Get started topic.

c. Open the Mouse and keyboard: What's new topic, then read the Help information on that topic.

d. In the Search Help text box, search for help about user accounts.

e. Find the link that describes how to create a user account, then click it.

f. Read the topic, clicking links as necessary, then close the Windows Help and Support window.

9. Exit Windows 8.

a. Shut down your computer using the Shut down command or the preferred command for your work or school setting.

b. Turn off your monitor if necessary.

Independent Challenge 1

You work for Will's Percussion, a Maine manufacturer of drums and drumsticks. The company ships percussion instruments and supplies to music stores and musicians in the United States and Canada. The owner, Will, wants to know an easy way for his employees to learn about the new features of Windows 8, and he has asked you to help.

a. Start your computer, log on to Windows 8 if necessary, then open Windows Help and Support.

b. Search Help for the text **what's new**.

c. Click the Get to know Windows 8 link.

d. Scroll the results window to see its contents, then scroll back to the top.

e. Using pencil and paper, or the WordPad app if you wish, write a short memo to Will summarizing, in your own words, three important new features in Windows 8. If you used WordPad to write the memo, use the Print button to print the document, then use the Exit command on the File tab to close WordPad without saving your changes to the document.

f. Close the Windows Help and Support window, then exit Windows and shut down.

Independent Challenge 2

You are the new manager for Katharine Anne's Designs, a business that supplies floral arrangements to New York businesses. The company maintains four delivery vans that supply flowers to various locations. Katharine asks you to investigate how the Windows 8 Calculator accessory can help her company be a responsible energy consumer.

a. Start your computer, log on to Windows 8 if necessary, then open the Windows 8 accessory called Calculator.

b. Click to enter the number 87 on the Calculator.

c. Click the division sign (/) button.

FIGURE A-27

d. Click the number 2.

e. Click the equals sign button (=), and write down the result shown in the Calculator window. (*Hint:* The result should be 43.5.) See **FIGURE A-27**.

f. Click the Help menu in the Calculator window, then click View Help. Locate the Calculator: Frequently asked questions topic, and scroll down to locate information on how to calculate fuel economy. Follow the instructions, and perform at least one calculation of fuel economy.

g. Start WordPad, write a short memo about how Calculator can help you calculate fuel consumption, print the document using the Print command on the File tab, then exit WordPad without saving.

h. Close the Help window.

i. Close the Calculator, then exit Windows.

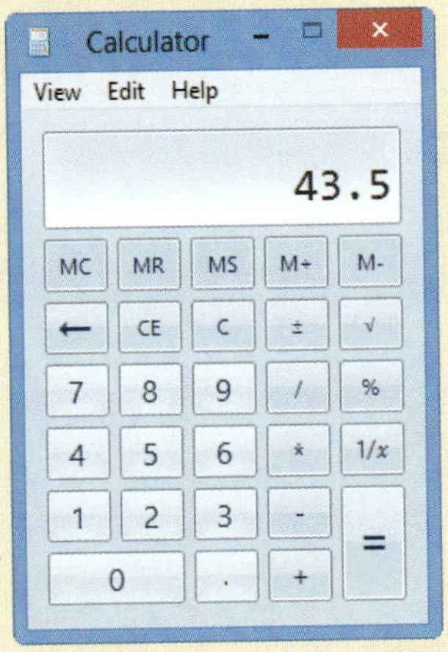

Independent Challenge 3

You are the office manager for Eric's Pet Shipping, a service business in Seattle, Washington, that specializes in air shipping of cats and dogs across the United States and Canada. It's important to know the temperature in the destination city, so the animals won't be in danger from extreme temperatures when they are unloaded from the aircraft. Eric has asked you to find a way to easily monitor temperatures in destination cities. You decide to use a Windows app so you can see current temperatures in Celsius on your desktop. (*Note:* To complete the steps below, your computer must be connected to the Internet.)

a. Start your computer and sign in to Windows 8 if necessary, then at the Start screen, click the Weather app.

b. If multiple locations appear, click one of your choice.

c. Right-click the sky area above the weather information, then in the bar at the top of the screen, click Places.

d. Click the plus sign, click in the Enter Location text box if necessary, then type **Vancouver**.

e. Click Vancouver, British Columbia, Canada, in the drop-down list. Vancouver, Canada, is added to your Places Favorites.

f. Add another location that interests you.

g. Close the apps and return to the Start screen.

h. Open WordPad, write Eric a memo outlining how you can use the Windows Weather app to help keep pets safe, print the memo if you wish, close WordPad, then exit Windows.

Independent Challenge 4: Explore

As a professional photographer, you often evaluate pictures. You decide to explore the Windows Photo app so you can access pictures from various online sources. (*Note:* To complete the steps below, your computer must be connected to the Internet.)

a. Start your computer and sign in to Windows 8 if necessary, then click to open the Photos app.

b. Explore any picture that may have been downloaded from your Windows SkyDrive account, Facebook, or Flickr. (*Note:* You might need to sign into your Microsoft account in order to access some locations.)

c. Right-click any area of the Photo app screen, then explore what this allows you to do.

d. Add three pictures to your Pictures library.

e. Click OK.

Visual Workshop

Using the skills you've learned in this unit, open and arrange elements on your screen so it looks similar to **FIGURE A-28** (the date and time will differ). Note the position of the Recycle Bin, the size and location of the Paint window and the Help and Support window, and the presence of the Charms bar. Open WordPad and write a paragraph summarizing how you used pointing, clicking, and dragging to make your screen look like **FIGURE A-28**. Print your work if you wish, exit WordPad without saving changes to the document, then shut down Windows.

FIGURE A-28

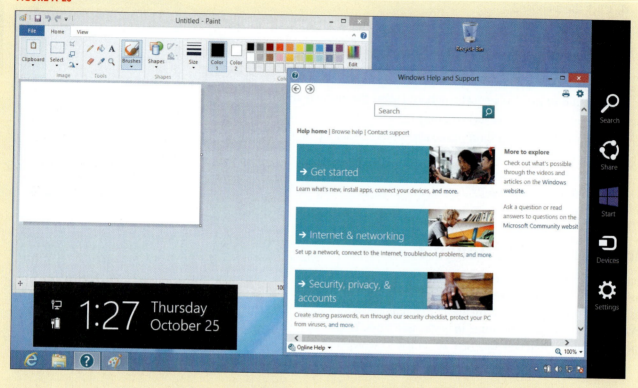

Understanding File Management

CASE ▶ Now that you are familiar with the Windows 8 operating system, your new employer has asked you to become familiar with **file management**, or how to create, save, locate and delete the files you create with Windows application programs. You begin by reviewing how files are organized on your computer, and then begin working with files you create in the WordPad app.

Unit Objectives

After completing this unit, you will be able to:

- Understand files and folders
- Create and save a file
- Explore the files and folders on your computer
- Change file and folder views

- Open, edit, and save files
- Copy files
- Move and rename files
- Search for files, folders, and programs
- Delete and restore files

Files You Will Need

No files needed.

Understand Files and Folders

Learning Outcomes
• Analyze a file hierarchy
• Examine files and folders

As you work with computer programs, you create and save files, such as letters, drawings, or budgets. When you save files, you usually save them inside folders to help keep them organized. The files and folders on your computer are organized in a **file hierarchy**, a system that arranges files and folders in different levels, like the branches of a tree. **FIGURE B-1** shows a sample file hierarchy. **CASE** *You decide to use folders and files to organize the information on your computer.*

DETAILS

Use the following guidelines as you organize files using your computer's file hierarchy:

• ### Use folders and subfolders to organize files

As you work with your computer, you can add folders to your hierarchy and name them to help you organize your work. As you've learned, folders are storage areas in which you can group related files. You should give folders unique names that help you easily identify them. You can also create **subfolders**, which are folders that are inside other folders. Windows 8 comes with several existing folders, such as My Documents, My Music, My Pictures, and My Videos, that you can use as a starting point.

• ### View and manage files in File Explorer

You can view and manage your computer contents using a built-in program called **File Explorer**, shown in **FIGURE B-2**. A File Explorer window is divided into **panes**, or sections. The **Navigation pane** on the left side of the window shows the folder structure on your computer. When you click a folder in the Navigation pane, you see its contents in the **File list** on the right side of the window. To open File Explorer from the desktop, click the File Explorer button 📁 on the taskbar. To open it from the Start screen, begin typing File Explorer, and when you see the program name on the Apps screen, press [Enter].

QUICK TIP
The program name "File Explorer" doesn't appear in the title bar. Instead, you'll see the current folder name.

• ### Understand file addresses

A window also contains an **Address bar**, an area just below the Ribbon that shows the address, or location, of the files that appear in the File list. An **address** is a sequence of folder names, separated by the ▶ symbol, which describes a file's location in the file hierarchy. An address shows the folder with the highest hierarchy level on the left and steps through each hierarchy level toward the right; this is sometimes called a **path**. For example, the My Documents folder might contain subfolders named Work and Personal. If you clicked the Personal folder in the File list, the Address bar would show My Documents ▶ Personal. Each location between the ▶ symbols represents a level in the file hierarchy. The same path appears in the window's title bar, but instead of ▶ between the hierarchy levels, you see the backslash symbol (\ ). If you see a file path written out, you'll most likely see it with backslashes. For example, in Figure B-1, if you wanted to write the path to the Honolulu Sunset photo file, you would write My Documents\Quest Specialty Travel\Photos\Honolulu Sunset.jpg. File addresses might look complicated if they may have many levels, but they are helpful because they always describe the exact location of a file or folder in a file hierarchy.

QUICK TIP
Remember that in the Address bar you single-click a folder or subfolder to show its contents, but in the File list you double-click it.

• ### Navigate up and down using the Address bar and File list

You can use the Address bar and the File list to move up or down in the hierarchy one or more levels at a time. To **navigate up** in your computer's hierarchy, you can click a folder or subfolder name to the left of the current folder name in the Address bar. For example, in **FIGURE B-2**, you can move up in the hierarchy one level by clicking once on Users in the Address bar. Then the File list would show the subfolders and files inside the Users folder. To **navigate down** in the hierarchy, double-click a subfolder in the File list. The path in the Address bar then shows the path to that subfolder.

• ### Navigate up and down using the Navigation pane

You can also use the Navigation pane to navigate among folders. Move the mouse pointer over the Navigation pane, then click the small triangles to the left of a folder name to show ▷ or hide ◢ the folder's contents under the folder name. Subfolders appear indented under the folders that contain them, showing that they are inside that folder.

Understanding File Management

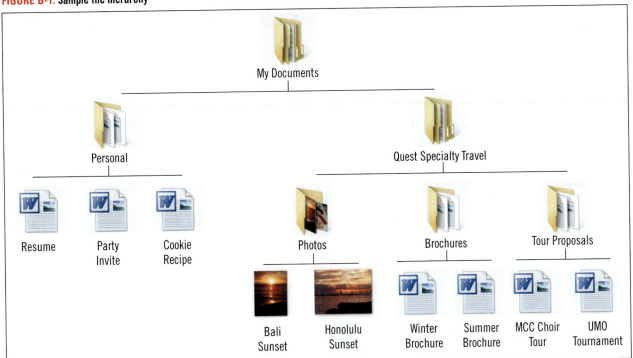

FIGURE B-2: File Explorer window

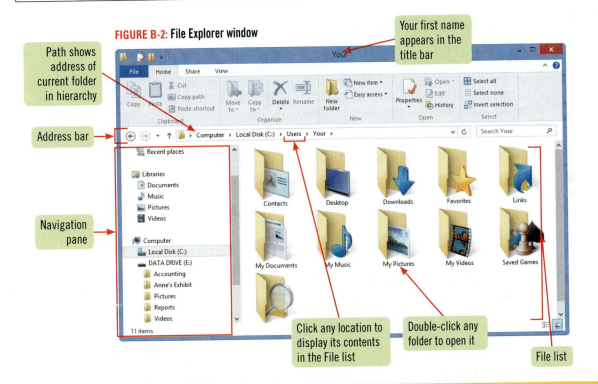

Plan your file organization

As you manage your files, you should plan how you want to organize them. First, identify the types of files you work with, such as images, music, and documents. Think about the content, such as personal, business, clients, or projects. Then think of a folder organization that will help you find them later. For example, you can use subfolders in the My Pictures folder to separate family photos from business photos or to group them by location

or by month. In the My Documents folder, you might group personal files in one subfolder and business files in another subfolder. Then create additional subfolders to further separate sets of files. You can always move files among folders and rename folders. You should periodically reevaluate your folder structure to make sure it continues to meet your needs.

Create and Save a File

**Learning
Outcomes:**
• Start WordPad
• Create a file
• Save a file

After you start a program and create a new file, the file exists only in your computer's **random access memory (RAM)**, a temporary storage location. RAM contains information only when your computer is on. When you turn off your computer, it automatically clears the contents of RAM. So you need to save a new file onto a storage device that permanently stores the file so you can open, change, and use it later. One important storage device is your computer's hard drive built into your computer. Another popular option is a **USB flash drive**, a small, portable storage device. **CASE** ▶ *You create a document, then save it.*

STEPS

1. **At the Start screen, type** word

   Available apps with "word" in their names are listed. See **FIGURE B-3**.

2. **Click** WordPad, **then maximize the WordPad window if necessary**

   Near the top of the WordPad window you see the Ribbon containing command buttons, similar to those you used in Paint in Unit A. The Home tab appears in front. A new, blank document appears in the document window. The blinking insertion point shows you where the next character you type will appear.

3. **Type** New Tours, **then press** [Enter] **twice, type** Thailand, **press** [Enter], **type** New Zealand, **press** [Enter], **type** Canada, **press** [Enter] **twice, then type your name**

   See **FIGURE B-4**.

4. **Click the** File tab, **then click** Save

   The first time you save a file using the Save button, the Save As dialog box opens. You use this dialog box to name the file and choose a storage location for it. The Save As dialog box has many of the same elements as a File Explorer window, including an Address bar, a Navigation pane, and a File list. Below the Address bar, the **toolbar** contains command buttons you can click to perform actions. In the Address bar, you can see the Documents library (which includes the My Documents folder) is the **default**, or automatically selected, storage location. But you can easily change it.

5. **Plug your USB flash drive into a USB port on your computer, if necessary**

6. **In the Navigation pane scroll bar, click the** down scroll arrow ☑ **as needed to see Computer and any storage devices listed under it**

   Under Computer, you see the storage locations available on your computer, such as Local Disk (C:) (your hard drive) and Removable Disk (F:) (your USB drive name and letter might differ). These storage locations are like folders in that you can open them and store files in them.

7. **Click the name for your USB flash drive**

   The files and folders on your USB drive, if any, appear in the File list. The Address bar shows the location where the file will be saved, which is now Computer ▶ Removable Disk (F:) (or the name of your drive). You need to give your document a meaningful name so you can find it later.

8. **Click in the** File name text box **to select the default name** Document.rtf, **type** New Tours, **compare your screen to** FIGURE B-5, **then click** Save

   The document is saved as a file on your USB flash drive. The filename New Tours.rtf appears in the title bar. The ".rtf" at the end of the filename is the file extension that Windows 8 added automatically. A **file extension** is a three- or four-letter sequence, preceded by a period, which identifies a file to your computer, in this case **Rich Text Format**. The WordPad program creates files in RTF format.

9. **Click the** Close button ❌ **on the WordPad window**

   The WordPad program closes. Your New Tours document is now saved in the location you specified.

FIGURE B-3: Results list

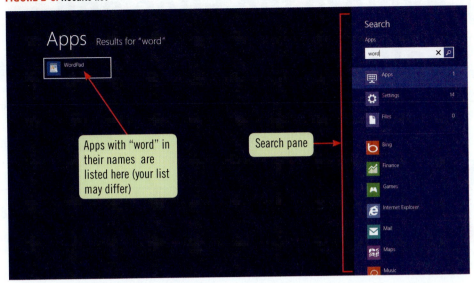

Apps with "word" in their names are listed here (your list may differ)

Search pane

FIGURE B-4: New document in WordPad

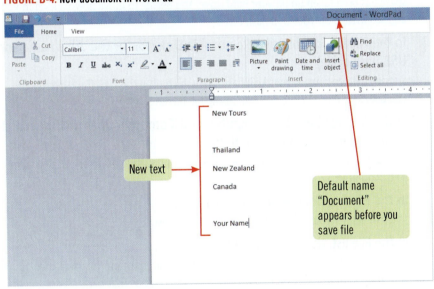

New text

Default name "Document" appears before you save file

FIGURE B-5: Save As dialog box

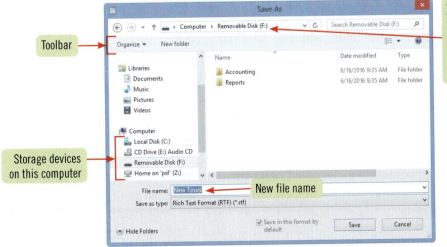

After you click Save, your New Tours.rtf document will be saved at this address (your drive name and letter will differ)

Toolbar

Storage devices on this computer

New file name

Explore the Files and Folders on Your Computer

In a File Explorer window, you can navigate through your computer contents using the File list, the Address bar, and the Navigation pane. Examining your computer and its existing folder and file structure helps you decide where to save files as you work with Windows 8 apps. **CASE** *In preparation for organizing documents at your new job, you look at the files and folders on your computer.*

STEPS

1. **If you see the Start screen, click the Desktop tile to display the Windows 8 desktop**

2. **On the taskbar, click the File Explorer button [icon], then in the File Explorer Navigation pane, click Computer**

   TROUBLE
   If you don't see the colored bar, click the View tab, then click Tiles in the Layout group.

   Your computer's storage devices appear in a window, as shown in **FIGURE B-6**. These include hard drives; devices with removable storage, such as CD and DVD drives or USB flash drives; portable devices such as personal digital assistants (PDAs); and any network storage locations. A colored bar shows you how much space has been taken up on your hard drive. You decide to move down a level in your computer's hierarchy and see what is on your USB flash drive.

3. **In the File list, double-click Removable Disk (F:) (or the drive name and letter for your USB flash drive)**

   TROUBLE
   If you do not have a USB flash drive, click the Documents library in the Navigation pane instead.

   You see the contents of your USB flash drive, including the New Tours.rtf file you saved in the last lesson. You decide to navigate one level up in the file hierarchy.

4. **In the Address bar, click Computer, or if Computer does not appear, click the far-left list arrow in the Address bar, then click Computer**

   You return to the Computer window showing your storage devices. You decide to look at the contents of your hard drive.

5. **In the File list, double-click Local Disk (C:)**

   The contents of your hard drive appear in the File list.

6. **In the File list, double-click the Users folder**

   The Users folder contains a subfolder for each user account on this computer. You might see a folder with your user account name on it. Each user's folder contains that person's documents. User folder names are the names that were used to log in when your computer was set up. When a user logs in, the computer allows that user access to the folder with the same user name. If you are using a computer with more than one user, you might not have permission to view other users' folders. There is also a Public folder that any user can open.

7. **Double-click the folder with your user name on it**

   Depending on how your computer is set up, this folder might be labeled with your name; however, if you are using a computer in a lab or a public location, your folder might be called Student or Computer User or something similar. You see a list of folders, such as My Documents, My Music, and others. See **FIGURE B-7**.

8. **Double-click My Documents in the File list**

   QUICK TIP
   In the Address bar, you can click ▶ to the right of a folder name to see a list of its subfolders; if the folder is open, its name appears in bold in the list.

   In the Address bar, the path to the My Documents folder is Computer ▶ Local Disk (C:) ▶ Users ▶ *Your User Name* ▶ My Documents.

9. **In the Navigation pane, click Computer**

   You once again see your computer's storage devices. You can also move up one level at a time in your file hierarchy by clicking the Up arrow ⬆ on the toolbar, or by pressing [Backspace] on your keyboard. See **TABLE B-1** for a summary of techniques for navigating through your computer's file hierarchy.

Understanding File Management

FIGURE B-6: Computer window showing storage devices

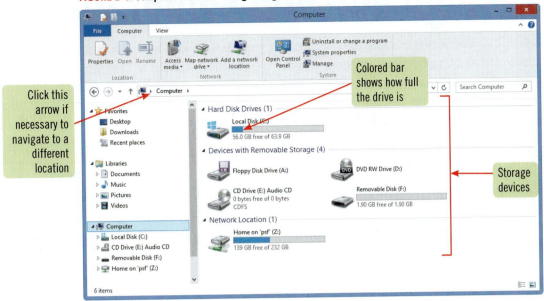

Click this arrow if necessary to navigate to a different location

Colored bar shows how full the drive is

Storage devices

FIGURE B-7: Your user name folder

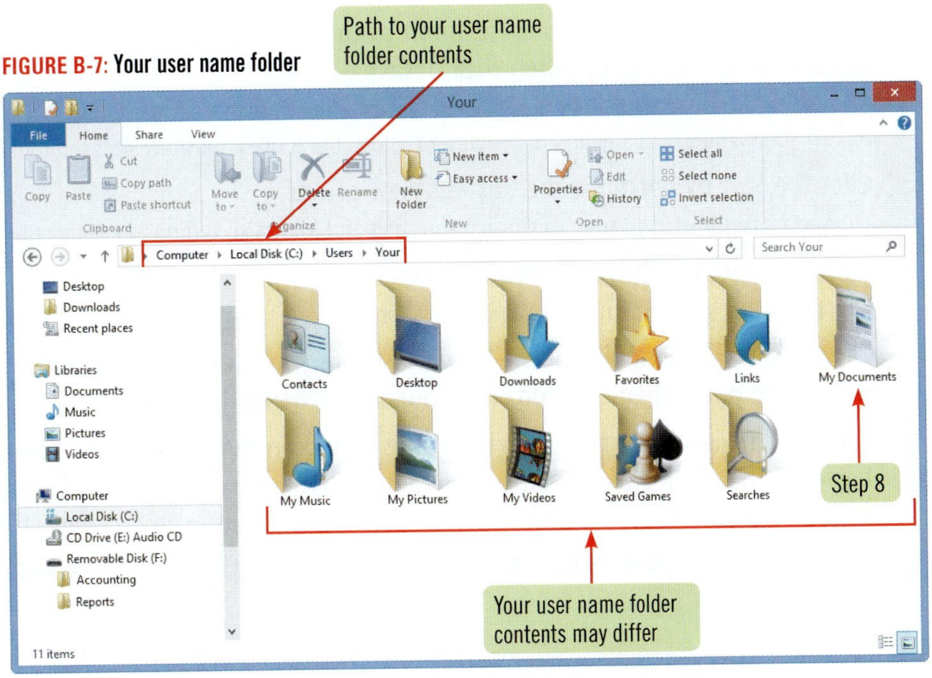

Path to your user name folder contents

Step 8

Your user name folder contents may differ

TABLE B-1: Navigating your computer's file hierarchy

to do this	Navigation pane	Address bar	File list	keyboard
Move up in hierarchy	Click a drive or folder name	Click an item to the left of ▶ or Click the **Up to** arrow ⬆		Press [**Backspace**]
Move down in hierarchy	Click a drive or folder name that is indented from the left	Click an item to the right of ▶	Double-click a folder	Press ⬆ or ⬇ to select a folder, then press [**Enter**] to open the selected folder
Return to previously viewed location		Click the **Back to** button ⬅ or **Forward to** button ➡		

Windows 8

Change File and Folder Views

As you view your folders and files, you can customize your **view**, which is a set of appearance choices for files and folders. Changing your view does not affect the content of your files or folders, only the way they appear. You can choose from eight different **layouts** to display your folders and files as different sized icons, or as a list. You can also change the order in which the folders and files appear. You can also show a preview of a file in the window. **CASE** *You experiment with different views of your folders and files.*

STEPS

1. **In the File Explorer window's Navigation pane, click Local Disk (C:), in the File list double-click Users, then double-click the folder with your user name**

   You opened your user name folder, which is inside the Users folder.

2. **Click the View tab on the Ribbon, then click the More button** ⩥ **in the Layout group**

   The list of available layouts appears, as shown in **FIGURE B-8**.

3. **Click Extra large icons in the Layout list**

   In this view, the folder items appear as very large icons in the File list. This layout is especially helpful for image files, because you can see what the pictures are without opening each one.

4. **On the View tab, in the Layout list, point to the other layouts while watching the appearance of the File list, then click Details**

   In Details view, shown in **FIGURE B-9**, you can see each item's name, the date it was modified, and its file type. It shows the size of any files in the current folder, but it does not show sizes for folders.

5. **Click the Sort by button in the Current view group**

   The Sort by menu lets you **sort**, or reorder, your files and folders according to several criteria.

6. **Click Descending if it is not already selected**

   Now the folders are sorted in reverse alphabetical order.

7. **Click Removable Disk (F:) (or the location where you store your Data Files) in the Navigation pane, then click the New Tours.rtf filename in the File list**

8. **Click the Preview pane button in the Panes group on the View tab if necessary**

   A preview of the selected New Tours.rtf file you created earlier in this unit appears in the Preview pane on the right side of the screen. The WordPad file is not open, but you can still see the file's contents. See **FIGURE B-10**.

9. **Click the Preview pane button again to close the pane, then click the window's Close button** ✕

Snapping Windows 8 apps

If your machine has a screen resolution of 1366 × 768 or higher, you can use snapping to view two Windows 8 apps side by side. Go to the Start screen and open the first app, then return to the Start screen and open the second app. Point to the upper-left corner of the screen until you can see a small square representing the first app, right-click the square, then click Snap left or Snap right. (Or you can drag the square to the right or left side of the screen.) One app then occupies one third of the screen and the other taking up two thirds of the screen. See **FIGURE B-11**.

FIGURE B-11: Using snapping to view Weather and SkyDrive apps

FIGURE B-8: Layout options for viewing folders and files

FIGURE B-9: Your user name folder contents in Details view

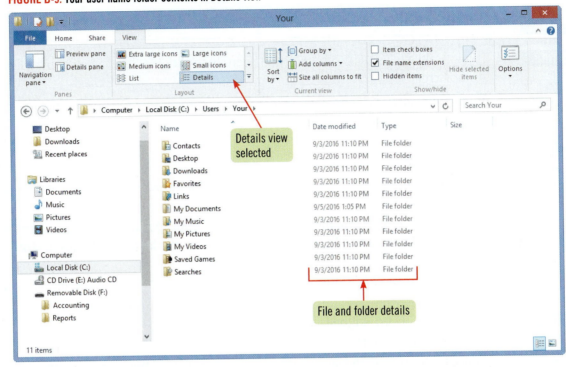

FIGURE B-10: Preview of selected New Tours.rtf file

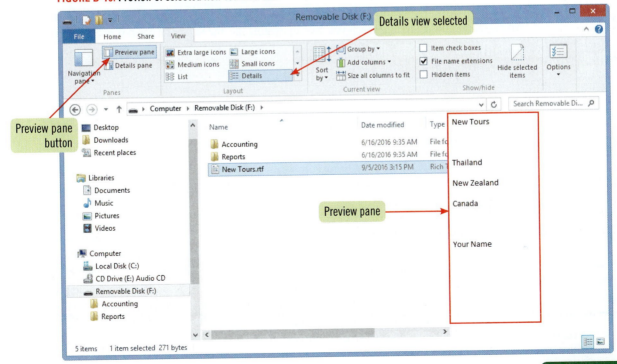

Open, Edit, and Save Files

Once you have created a file and saved it with a name to a storage location, you can easily open it and **edit** (make changes to) it. For example, you might want to add or delete text or add a picture. Then you save the file again so the file contains your latest changes. Usually you save a file with the same filename and in the same location as the original, which replaces the existing file with the most up-to-date version. To save a file you have changed, you use the Save command. **CASE** ▶ *You need to complete the list of new tours, so you need to open the new Tours file you created earlier.*

STEPS

1. **Point to the lower-left corner of the screen, then click the Start thumbnail to display the Start screen**

2. **Begin typing wordpad, then click the WordPad program if it is not selected or, if it is, simply press [Enter]**

   The WordPad program opens on the desktop.

3. **Click the File tab, then click Open**

   The Open dialog box opens. It contains a Navigation pane and a File list like the Save As dialog box and the File Explorer window.

4. **Scroll down in the Navigation pane if necessary until you see Computer and the list of computer drives, then click Removable Disk (F:) (or the location where you store your Data Files)**

   The contents of your USB flash drive (or the file storage location you chose) appear in the File list, as shown in **FIGURE B-12**.

5. **Click New Tours.rtf in the File list, then click Open**

   The document you created earlier opens.

6. **Click to the right of the last "a" in Canada, press [Enter], then type Greenland**

   The edited document includes the text you just typed. See **FIGURE B-13**.

7. **Click the File tab, then click Save, as shown in FIGURE B-14**

   WordPad saves the document with your most recent changes, using the filename and location you specified when you previously saved it. When you save an existing file, the Save As dialog box does not open.

8. **Click the File tab, then click Exit**

Comparing Save and Save As

The WordPad menu has two save command options—Save and Save As. The first time you save a file, the Save As dialog box opens (whether you choose Save or Save As). Here you can select the drive and folder where you want to save the file and enter its filename. If you edit a previously saved file, you can save the file to the same location with the same filename using the Save command. The Save command updates the stored file using the same location and filename without opening the Save As dialog box. In some situations, you might want to save a copy of the existing document using a different filename or in a different storage location. To do this, open the document, click the Save As command on the File tab, navigate to the location where you want to save the copy if necessary, and/or edit the name of the file.

FIGURE B-12: Navigating in the Open dialog box

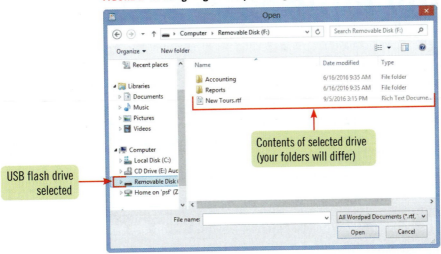

USB flash drive selected

Contents of selected drive (your folders will differ)

FIGURE B-13: Edited document

New Tours

Thailand

New Zealand

Canada

Greenland | ← Added text

Your Name

FIGURE B-14: Saving the updated document

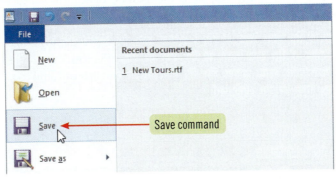

Save command

Using cloud storage

Many users store their files on special file storage locations on the World Wide Web, known as **cloud storage** locations. Examples of cloud storage locations include **Microsoft SkyDrive** and **DropBox**. By storing files in the cloud, your files are automatically updated when you make changes to them on your computer, and you can access them from different devices, including laptops, tablets, and smartphones. Microsoft Office programs such as Word and Excel show SkyDrive as a storage location when you open or save a file, making cloud storage a convenient option.

Understanding File Management

Copy Files

Learning Outcomes:
• Create a new folder
• Copy and paste a file

Sometimes you need to make a copy of an existing file. For example, you might want to put a copy on a USB flash drive so you can open the file on another machine or share it with a friend or colleague. Or you might want to create a copy as a **backup**, or replacement, in case something happens to your original file. You can copy files and folders using the Copy command and then place the copy in another location using the Paste command. You cannot have two copies of a file with the same name in the same folder. If you try to do this, Windows 8 asks you if you want to replace the first one, and then gives you a chance to give the second copy a different name. **CASE** ▶ *You want to create a backup copy of the New Tours document that you can store in a folder for company newsletter items. First you need to create the folder, then you can copy the file.*

STEPS

1. **On the desktop, click the File Explorer button 🗔 on the taskbar**

2. **In the Navigation pane, click Removable Disk (F:) (or the drive name and letter that represents the location where you store your Data Files)**
   First you create the new folder you plan to use for storing newsletter-related files.

QUICK TIP
You can also create a new folder by clicking the New Folder button on the Quick Access toolbar (on the left side of the title bar).

3. **If you don't see the Ribbon, double-click the Home tab to open the Ribbon**

4. **In the New group on the Home tab, click the New folder button**
   A new folder appears in the File list, with its default name, New folder, selected.

5. **Type Newsletter Items, then press [Enter]**
   Because the folder name was selected, the text you typed, Newsletter Items, replaced it. Pressing [Enter] confirmed your entry, and the folder is now named Newsletter Items.

QUICK TIP
You can also copy a file by right-clicking the file in the File list and then clicking Copy, or you can use the keyboard by pressing and holding [Ctrl], pressing [C], then releasing both keys.

6. **In the File list, click the New Tours.rtf document you saved earlier, then click the Copy button in the Clipboard group, as shown in FIGURE B-15**
   When you use the Copy command, Windows 8 places a duplicate copy of the file in an area of your computer's random access memory called the **clipboard**, ready to paste, or place, in a new location. Copying and pasting a file leaves the file in its original location.

7. **In the File list, double-click the Newsletter Items folder**
   The folder opens. Nothing appears in the File list because the folder currently is empty.

QUICK TIP
To paste using the keyboard, press and hold [Ctrl] and press [V], then release both keys.

8. **Click the Paste button in the Clipboard group**
   A copy of the New Tours.rtf file is pasted into the Newsletter Items folder. See **FIGURE B-16**. You now have two copies of the New Tours.rtf file: one on your USB flash drive in the main folder, and another in your new Newsletter Items folder. The file remains on the clipboard until you end your Windows session or place another item on the clipboard.

TABLE B-2: Selected Send to menu commands

menu option	use to
Compressed (zipped) folder	Create a new compressed (smaller) file with a .zip file extension
Desktop (create shortcut)	Create a shortcut (link) for the file on the desktop
Documents	Copy the file to the Documents library
Fax recipient	Send a file to a fax recipient
Mail recipient	Create an e-mail with the file attached to it (only if you have an e-mail program on your computer)
DVD RW Drive (D:)	Copy the file to your computer's DVD drive
Removable Disk (F:)	Copy the file to a removable disk drive (F:) (your drive letter may differ)

FIGURE B-15: Copying a file

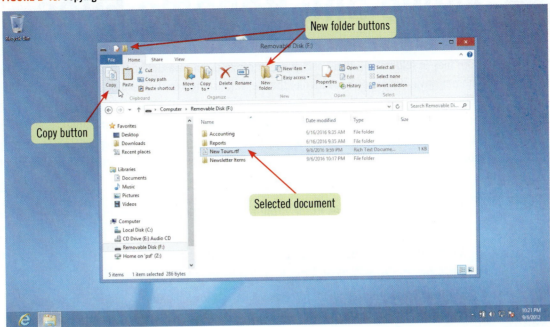

New folder buttons

Copy button

Selected document

FIGURE B-16: Duplicate file pasted into Newsletter Items folder

Copy is pasted in Newsletter Items folder

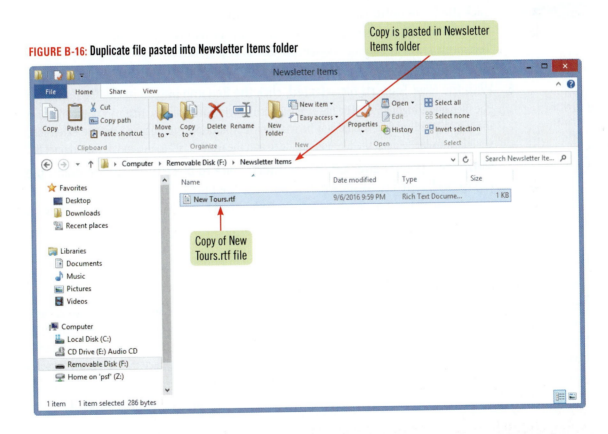

Copy of New Tours.rtf file

Copying files using Send to

You can also copy and paste a file using the Send to command. In File Explorer, right-click the file you want to copy, point to Send to, then in the shortcut menu, click the name of the device you want to send a copy of the file to. This leaves the original file on your hard drive and creates a copy on the external device. You can send a file to a compressed file, the desktop, a mail recipient, your Documents library, or a drive on your computer. See **TABLE B-2**.

Move and Rename Files

Learning
Outcomes:
• Cut and paste
a file
• Rename a file

As you work with files, you might need to move files or folders to another location. You can move one or more files or folders at a time, and you can move them to a different folder on the same drive or to a different drive. When you **move** a file, the file is transferred to the new location, and unlike copying it no longer exists in its original location. You can move a file using the Cut and Paste commands. Before or after you move a file, you might find that you want to change its name. You can easily rename it to make the name more descriptive or accurate. **CASE** ▶ *You decide to move your original New Tours.rtf document to your Documents library. After you move it, you edit the filename so it better describes the file contents.*

STEPS

QUICK TIP
You can also cut a file by right-clicking it in the File list, then clicking Cut, or by clicking it, pressing and holding [Ctrl] on the keyboard, pressing [X], then releasing both keys.

1. **In the Address bar, click Removable Disk (F:) (or the drive name and letter for your USB flash drive)**

2. **Click the New Tours.rtf document to select it**

3. **Click the Cut button in the Clipboard group on the Ribbon**
   The icon representing the cut file becomes lighter in color, indicating you have cut it, as shown in **FIGURE B-17**.

4. **In the Navigation Pane, under Libraries, click Documents**
   You navigated to your Documents Library.

QUICK TIP
You can also paste a file by right-clicking an empty area in the File list and then clicking Paste, or by pressing and holding [Ctrl] on the keyboard, pressing [V], then releasing both keys.

5. **Click the Paste button in the Clipboard group**
   The New Tours.rtf document appears in your Documents library and remains selected. See **FIGURE B-18**. Documents you paste into your Documents library are automatically stored in your My Documents folder. The filename could be clearer, to help you remember that it contains a list of new tours.

6. **With the New Tours.rtf file selected, click the Rename button in the Organize group**
   The filename is highlighted. The file extension isn't highlighted because that part of the filename identifies the file to WordPad and should not be changed. If you deleted or changed the file extension, WordPad would be unable to open the file. You decide to add the word "List" to the end of the original filename.

7. **Move the ⌶ pointer after the "s" in "Tours", click to place the insertion point, press [Spacebar], type List as shown in FIGURE B-19, then press [Enter]**
   You changed the name of the pasted file in the Documents library. The filename now reads New Tours List.rtf.

8. **Close the window**

Using Windows 8 libraries

The Navigation pane contains not only files and folders, but also libraries. A **library** gathers file and folder locations from different locations on your computer and displays them in one location. For example, you might have pictures in several different folders on your storage devices. You can add these folder locations to your Pictures library. Then when you want to see all your pictures, you open your Pictures library instead of several different folders. The picture files stay in their original locations, but their names appear in the Pictures library. A library is not a folder that stores files, but rather a way of viewing similar types of documents that you have stored in multiple locations on your computer. **FIGURE B-20** shows the four libraries that come with Windows 8: Documents, Music, Pictures, and Videos. To help you distinguish between library locations and actual folder

locations, library names differ from actual folder names. For example, the My Documents folder is on your hard drive, but the library name is Documents. If you save a document to the Documents library, it is automatically saved to your My Documents folder.

FIGURE B-20: Libraries that come with Windows 8

Documents   Music   Pictures   Videos

FIGURE B-17: Cutting a file

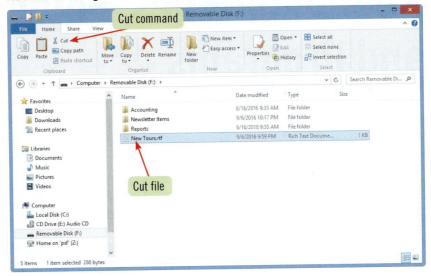

FIGURE B-18: Pasted file in Documents library

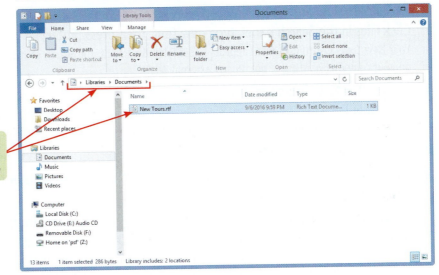

FIGURE B-19: Renaming a file

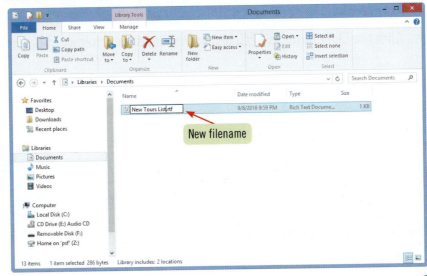

Understanding File Management

Learning Outcomes:
• Search for a file
• Open a found file

Search for Files, Folders, and Programs

Windows Search helps you quickly find any program, folder, or file. You can search from the Start screen using the Charms bar to locate applications, settings, or files. To search a particular location on your computer, you can use the Search box in File Explorer. You enter search text by typing one or more letter sequences or words that help Windows identify the item you want. The search text you type is called your **search criteria**. Your search criteria can be a filename, part of a filename, or any other text. **CASE** *You want to locate the New Tours.rtf document so you can print it for a colleague.*

STEPS

1. **Move the pointer to the lower-left corner of the screen, then click the Start thumbnail**
   The Start screen opens.

2. **Point to the upper-right corner of the screen, then point to and click the Search charm**
   A listing of the apps on your computer appears, along with a Search pane on the right side of the screen. See **FIGURE B-21**. You can search for Apps, Settings, or Files. Apps is selected by default.

   QUICK TIP
   To immediately open File search in the Search charm, press ⊞ [F].

3. **Click Files in the Search panel, type new tour, then press [Enter]**
   Your New Tours List.rtf document appears under Files. By default, the Search charm finds only files located on your computer hard drive, not on any external drives.

   QUICK TIP
   If you navigated to a specific folder in your file hierarchy, Windows would search that folder and any subfolders below it.

4. **Point to the New Tours List.rtf file**
   The path in the ScreenTip, C:\Users\Your Name\My Documents, indicates the found file is in the My Documents folder on the C: drive, as shown in **FIGURE B-22**.

5. **Press ⊞ twice to display the desktop**

6. **Click the File Explorer button 📁 on the taskbar, then click Computer in the Navigation pane**

   QUICK TIP
   Windows search is not case-sensitive, meaning that you can type upper- or lowercase letters when you search, and obtain the same results.

7. **Click in the Search box to the right of the Address bar, type new tour, then press [Enter]**
   Windows searches your computer for files that contain the words "new tour". A green bar in the Address bar indicates the progress of your search. After a few moments, your search results, shown in **FIGURE B-23**, appear. Windows found both the renamed file, New Tours List.rtf, in your My Documents folder, and the original New Tours.rtf document on your removable drive, in the Newsletter Items folder.

8. **Double-click the New Tours.rtf document on your removable flash drive**
   The file opens in WordPad or in another word-processing program on your computer that reads RTF files.

9. **Click the Close button ✕ on the WordPad (or other word-processor) window**

Using the Search Tools tab in File Explorer

The **Search Tools tab** appears in the Ribbon as soon as you click the Search text box, and it lets you narrow your search criteria. Use the commands in the Location group to specify a particular search location. The Refine group lets you limit the search to files modified after a certain date, or to files of a particular kind, size, type, or other property. The Options group lets you repeat previous searches, save searches, and open the folder containing a found file. See **FIGURE B-24**.

FIGURE B-24: Search Tools tab

FIGURE B-21: Apps screen and search pane

FIGURE B-22: Viewing the location of a found file

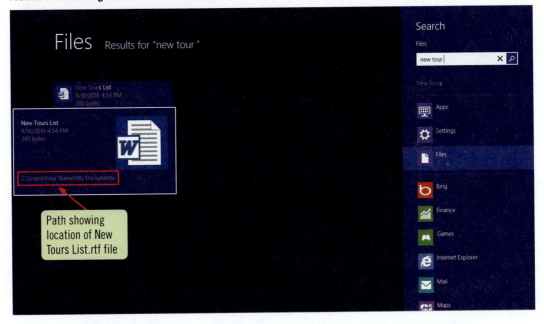

FIGURE B-23: Search results in File Explorer

Understanding File Management

Delete and Restore Files

Learning
Outcomes:
• Delete a file
• Restore a file
• Empty the
  Recycle Bin

If you no longer need a folder or file, you can delete (or remove) it from the storage device. By regularly deleting files and folders you no longer need and emptying the Recycle Bin, you free up valuable storage space on your computer. Windows 8 places folders and files you delete from your hard drive in the Recycle Bin. If you delete a folder, Windows 8 removes the folder as well as all files and subfolders stored in it. If you later discover that you need a deleted file or folder, you can restore it to its original location, as long as you have not yet emptied the Recycle Bin. Emptying the Recycle Bin permanently removes deleted folders and files from your computer. However, files and folders you delete from a removable drive, such as a USB flash drive, do not go to the Recycle Bin. They are immediately and permanently deleted and cannot be restored. **CASE** *You decide to delete the New Tours document, but later you change your mind about this.*

STEPS

1. **Click the Documents library in the File Explorer Navigation pane**

   Your Documents library opens, along with the Library Tools Manage tab on the Ribbon.

QUICK TIP
The Library Tools Manage tab becomes available on the Ribbon whenever a Library location is open. You can use it to change the locations the Library represents, as well as other related options.

2. **Click New Tours List.rtf to select it, then click the Delete list arrow in the Organize group on the Library Tools Manage tab; if the Show recycle confirmation command does not have a check mark next to it, click Show recycle confirmation (or if it does have a check mark, click the Delete list arrow again to close the menu)**

   Selecting the Show recycle confirmation command tells Windows that whenever you click the Delete button, you want to see a confirmation dialog box before Windows deletes the file. That way you can change your mind if you want, before deleting the file.

3. **Click the Delete button**

   The Delete File dialog box opens so you can confirm the deletion, as shown in **FIGURE B-25**.

4. **Click Yes**

   You deleted the file. Because the file was stored on your computer and not on a removable drive, it was moved to the Recycle Bin.

QUICK TIP
If the Recycle Bin icon does not contain crumpled paper, then it is empty.

5. **Click the Minimize button** – **on the window's title bar, examine the Recycle Bin icon, then double-click the Recycle Bin icon on the desktop**

   The Recycle Bin icon appears to contain crumpled paper, indicating that it contains deleted folders and/or files. The Recycle Bin window displays any previously deleted folders and files, including the New Tours List.rtf file.

6. **Click the New Tours List.rtf file to select it, then click the Restore the selected items button in the Restore group on the Recycle Bin Tools Manage tab, as shown in FIGURE B-26**

   The file returns to its original location and no longer appears in the Recycle Bin window.

7. **In the Navigation pane, click the Documents library**

   The Documents library window contains the restored file. You decide to permanently delete this file.

QUICK TIP
Another way to delete a file completely is to select the file, press and hold [Shift], then press [Delete]; if you click Yes in the message box that opens, Windows 8 deletes the file without sending it to the Recycle Bin. Use caution, because you cannot restore the file.

8. **Click the file New Tours List.rtf, click the Delete list arrow in the Organize group on the Library Tools Manage tab, click Permanently delete, then click Yes in the Delete File dialog box**

9. **Minimize the window, double-click the Recycle Bin, notice that the New Tours List.rtf file is no longer there, then close all open windows**

FIGURE B-25: Delete File dialog box

FIGURE B-26: Restoring a file from the Recycle Bin

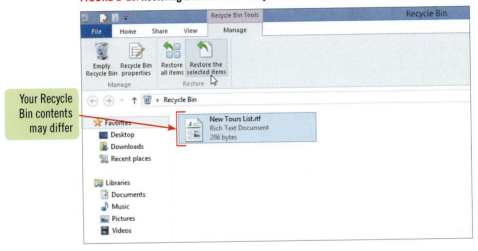

Your Recycle Bin contents may differ

More techniques for selecting and moving files

To select a group of items that are next to each other in a window, click the first item in the group, press and hold [Shift], then click the last item in the group. Both items you click and all the items between them become selected. To select files that are not next to each other, click the first file, press and hold [Ctrl], then click the other items you want to select as a group. Then you can copy, cut, or delete the group of files or folders you selected. **Drag and drop** is a technique in which you use your pointing device to drag a file or folder into a different folder and then drop it, or let go of the mouse button, to place it in that folder. Using drag and drop does not copy your file to the clipboard. If you drag and drop a file to a folder on a different drive, Windows 8 *copies the file*. However, if you drag and drop a file to a folder on the same drive, Windows 8 *moves* the file into that

folder instead. See **FIGURE B-27**. If you want to move a file to another drive, hold down [Shift] while you drag and drop. If you want to copy a file to another folder on the same drive, hold down [Ctrl] while you drag and drop.

FIGURE B-27: Moving a file using drag and drop

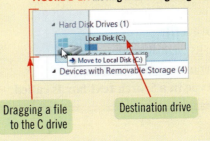

Dragging a file to the C drive

Destination drive

Understanding File Management

Practice

Concepts Review

Label the elements of the Windows 8 window shown in FIGURE B-28.

FIGURE B-28

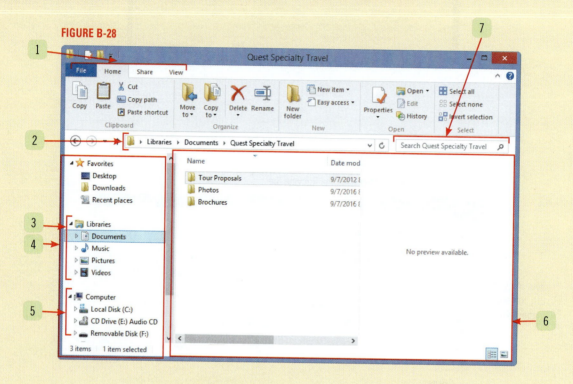

Match each term with the statement that best describes it.

8. File management
9. File extension
10. Address bar
11. Path
12. Library
13. File hierarchy

a. An area above the Files list that contains a path
b. Structure of files and folders organized in different levels
c. A series of locations separated by small triangles or backslashes that describes a file's location in the file hierarchy
d. Skills that help you organize your files and folders
e. A three- or four-letter sequence, preceded by a period, that identifies the type of file
f. Gathers files and folders from different computer locations

Select the best answer from the list of choices.

14. Which part of a window lets you see a file's contents without opening the file?

a. File list
b. Preview pane
c. Navigation pane
d. Address bar

15. When you move a file:

a. It remains in its original location.
b. It is no longer in its original location.
c. It is copied to another location.
d. It is no longer in your file hierarchy.

16. The text you type in a Search text box is called:

a. Search criteria.
b. RAM.
c. Sorting.
d. Clipboard.

17. Which of the following is not a visible section in a File Explorer window?
- **a.** Address bar
- **b.** File list
- **c.** Navigation pane
- **d.** Clipboard

18. The way your files appear in the Files list is determined by the:
- **a.** Path.
- **b.** View.
- **c.** Subfolder.
- **d.** Criterion.

19. When you copy a file, it is automatically placed in the:
- **a.** Preview pane.
- **b.** My Documents folder.
- **c.** Hierarchy.
- **d.** Clipboard.

20. After you delete a file from your hard disk, it is automatically placed in the:
- **a.** USB flash drive.
- **b.** Clipboard.
- **c.** Recycle Bin.
- **d.** Search box.

Skills Review

1. Understand files and folders.
- **a.** Create a file hierarchy for a property management business. The business manages three apartment buildings and two private homes. Activities include renting the properties and managing maintenance and repair. How would you organize your folders and files using a file hierarchy of at least three levels? How would you use folders and subfolders to keep the documents related to these activities distinct and easy to navigate? Draw a diagram and write a short paragraph explaining your answer.
- **b.** Use tools in the File Explorer window to create the folder hierarchy in the My Documents folder on your computer.

2. Create and save a file.
- **a.** Connect your USB flash drive to a USB port on your computer, then open WordPad from the Start screen.
- **b.** Type **Tour Marketing Plan** as the title, then start a new line.
- **c.** Type your name, then press [Enter] twice.
- **d.** Create the following list:

  Airline co-marketing

  Email blasts

  Web ads

  Adult education partnership
- **e.** Save the WordPad file with the filename **Tour Marketing Plan.rtf** on your USB flash drive.
- **f.** View the filename in the WordPad title bar, then close WordPad.

3. Explore the files and folders on your computer.
- **a.** Open a File Explorer window.
- **b.** Use the Navigation pane to navigate to your USB flash drive or another location where you store your Data Files.
- **c.** Use the Address bar to navigate to Computer.
- **d.** Use the File list to navigate to your local hard drive (C:).
- **e.** Use the File list to open the Users folder, and then open the folder that represents your user name.
- **f.** Open the My Documents folder. (*Hint:* The path is Computer\Local Disk (C:) \Users \Your User Name\ My Documents.)
- **g.** Use the Navigation pane to navigate back to your Computer contents.

4. Change file and folder views.
- **a.** Navigate to your USB flash drive using the method of your choice.
- **b.** Use the View tab to view its contents as large icons.
- **c.** View the drive contents in the seven other views.
- **d.** Sort the items on your USB flash drive by date modified in ascending order.
- **e.** Open the Preview pane, then view the selected item's preview.
- **f.** Close the Preview pane.

5. Open, edit, and save files.

   a. Open WordPad.

   b. Use the Open dialog box to open the Tour Marketing Plan.rtf document you created.

   c. After the text "Adult education partnership," add a line with the text **Travel conventions**.

   d. Save the document and close WordPad.

6. Copy files.

   a. In the File Explorer window, navigate to your USB flash drive if necessary.

   b. Copy the Tour Marketing Plan.rtf document.

   c. Create a new folder named **Marketing** on your USB flash drive or the location where you store your Data Files (*Hint:* Use the Home tab), then open the folder.

   d. Paste the document copy in the new folder.

7. Move and rename files.

   a. Navigate to your USB flash drive or the location where you store your Data Files.

   b. Select the Tour Marketing Plan.rtf document located there, then cut it.

   c. Navigate to your Documents library, then paste the file there.

   d. Rename the file **Tour Marketing Plan - Backup.rtf**.

8. Search for files, folders, and programs.

   a. Go to the Start screen, and use the Search charm to search for a file using the search text **backup**.

   b. Point to the found file, and notice its path.

   c. Open the Tour Marketing Plan - Backup document from the search results, then close WordPad. (*Hint:* Closing the program automatically closes any open documents.)

   d. Open a File Explorer window, click in the Search box, then use the Data Modified button on the Search Tools Search tab to find a file modified today. (*Hint:* Click the Date Modified button, then click Today.)

   e. Open the found document from the File list, then close WordPad.

9. Delete and restore files.

   a. Navigate to your Documents library.

   b. Verify that your Delete preference is Show recycle confirmation, then delete the Tour Marketing Plan Backup.rtf file.

   c. Open the Recycle Bin, and restore the document to its original location.

   d. Navigate to your Documents library, then move the Tour Marketing Plan-Backup.rtf file to your USB flash drive.

Independent Challenge 1

To meet the needs of pet owners in your town, you have opened a pet-sitting business named CritterCare. Customers hire you to care for their pets in their own homes when the pet owners go on vacation. To promote your new business, your Web site designer asks you to give her selling points to include in a Web ad.

   a. Connect your USB flash drive to your computer, if necessary.

   b. Create a new folder named **CritterCare** on your USB flash drive or the location where you store your Data Files.

   c. In the CritterCare folder, create two subfolders named **Print Ads** and **Web site**.

   d. Use WordPad to create a short paragraph or list that describes three advantages of your business. Use CritterCare as the first line, followed by the paragraph or list. Include an address and a phone number. Below the paragraph, type your name.

   e. Save the WordPad document with the filename **Selling Points.rtf** in the Web site folder, then close the document and exit WordPad.

   f. Open a File Explorer window, then navigate to the Web site folder.

   g. View the contents in at least three different views, then choose the view option that you prefer.

   h. Copy the Selling Points.rtf file, then paste a copy in the Document library.

   i. Rename the copied file **Selling Points Backup.rtf**.

   j. Close the folder.

Independent Challenge 2

As a freelance editor for several international publishers, you depend on your computer to meet critical deadlines. Whenever you encounter a computer problem, you contact a computer consultant who helps you resolve the problem. This consultant has asked you to document, or keep records of, your computer's current settings.

a. Connect your USB flash drive to your computer, if necessary.

b. Open the Computer window so you can view information on your drives and other installed hardware.

c. View the window contents using three different views, then choose the one you prefer.

d. Open WordPad and create a document with the title **My Hardware Documentation** and your name on separate lines.

e. List the names of the hard drive (or drives), devices with removable storage, and any other hardware devices installed on the computer you are using. Also include the total size and amount of free space on your hard drive(s) and removable storage drive(s). (*Hint:* If you need to check the Computer window for this information, use the taskbar button for the Computer window to view your drives, then use the WordPad taskbar button to return to WordPad.)

f. Save the WordPad document with the filename **My Hardware Documentation** on your USB flash drive or the location where you store your Data Files.

g. Close WordPad, then preview your document in the Preview pane.

Independent Challenge 3

You are an attorney at Garcia, Buck, and Sato, a large law firm. You participate in your firm's community outreach program by speaking at career days in area high schools. You teach students about career opportunities available in the field of law. You want to create a folder structure on your USB flash drive to store the files for each session.

a. Connect your USB flash drive to your computer, then open the window for your USB flash drive or the location where you store your Data Files.

b. Create a folder named **Career Days**.

c. In the Career Days folder, create a subfolder named **Nearwater High**, then open the folder.

d. Close the Nearwater High folder window.

e. Use WordPad to create a document with the title **Career Areas** and your name on separate lines, and the following list of items:
Current Opportunities:
Attorney
Paralegal
Police Officer
Judge

f. Save the WordPad document with the filename **Careers.rtf** in the Nearwater High folder. (*Hint:* After you switch to your USB flash drive in the Save As dialog box, open the Career Days folder, then open the Nearwater High folder before saving the file.)

g. Close WordPad.

h. Open WordPad and the Careers document again, add **Court Reporter** to the bottom of the list, then save the file and close WordPad.

i. Using pencil and paper, draw a diagram of your new folder structure.

j. Use the Search method of your choice to search for the Careers document, then open the file, to search your computer using the search criterion **car**. Locate the Careers.rtf document in the list, then use the link to open the file.

k. Close the file.

Independent Challenge 4: Explore

Think of a hobby or volunteer activity that you do now, or one that you would like to start. You will use your computer to help you manage your plans or ideas for this activity.

a. Using paper and pencil, sketch a folder structure with at least two subfolders to contain your documents for this activity.

b. Connect your USB flash drive to your computer, then open the window for your USB flash drive.

c. Create the folder structure for your activity, using your sketch as a reference.

d. Think of at least three tasks that you can do to further your work in your chosen activity.

e. Go to the Windows 8 Start screen, click the Store app tile and scroll to explore the available app categories. Choose a category that might relate to your activity, and click the Top Free tile to see if any of these apps might help you. Click an app name to read its description. (*Note:* You do not need to install any apps.)

f. Close the Store app by dragging its top border to the bottom of the screen.

g. Start a new WordPad document. Add the title **Next Steps** at the top of the page and your name on the next line.

h. Below your name, list the three tasks, then write a paragraph on how Windows 8 apps might help you accomplish your tasks. Save the file in one of the folders created on your USB flash drive, with the title **To Do.rtf**.

i. Close WordPad, then open a File Explorer window for the folder where you stored the document.

j. Create a copy of the file, place the copied file in your documents library, then rename this file with a name you choose.

k. Delete the copied file from your Documents library.

l. Open the Recycle Bin window, then restore the copied file to the Documents library.

Visual Workshop

Create the folder structure shown in **FIGURE B-29** on your USB flash drive (or in another location if requested by your instructor). As you work, use WordPad to prepare a short summary of the steps you followed to create the folder structure. Add your name to the document, then save it as **Customer Support.rtf** on your USB Flash drive or the location where you store your Data Files.

FIGURE B-29

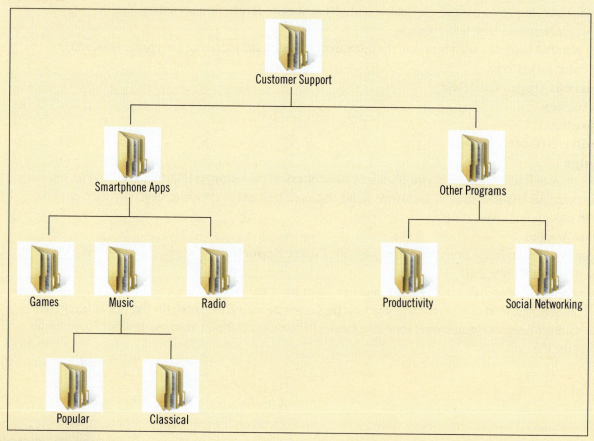

Glossary

Accessories Simple Windows application programs (apps) that perform specific tasks, such as the Calculator accessory for performing calculations. Also called Windows accessories.

Active window The window you are currently using; if multiple windows are open, the window with the darker title bar.

Address A sequence of drive and folder names that describes a folder's or file's location in the file hierarchy; the highest hierarchy level is on the left, with lower hierarchy levels separated by the ▶ symbol to its right.

Address bar In a window, the area just below the title bar that shows the file hierarchy, or address of the files that appear in the file list below it; the address appears as a series of links you can click to navigate to other locations on your computer.

App An application program; Windows 8 apps are designed to occupy the full screen and are available on the Start screen and at the Windows store. Desktop apps, such as Microsoft Office, open in resizable windows, and are available from many software companies.

App window The window that opens after you start an app, showing you the tools you need to use the program and any open program documents.

Application program Any program that lets you work with files or create and edit files such as graphics, letters, financial summaries, and other useful documents, as well as view Web pages on the Internet and send and receive e-mail. Also called an app.

Backup A duplicate copy of a file that is stored in another location.

Blog Web log, or a personal commentary on a website.

Border A window's edge; you can drag to resize the window.

Button A small rectangle you can click in order to issue a command to an application program.

Canvas In the Paint accessory, the area in the center of the app window that you use to create drawings.

Case sensitive An application program's (app's) ability to differentiate between uppercase and lowercase letters; usually used to describe how an operating system evaluates passwords that users type to gain entry to user accounts.

Charms bar A set of buttons that appear on the right side of the Windows 8 screen that let you find and send information, change your machine settings, and turn off your computer. When you display the Charms bar, the time and date appear on the left side of the screen.

Check box A box that turns an option on when checked or off when unchecked.

Click To quickly press and release the left button on the pointing device; also called single-click.

Clipboard A location in a computer's random access memory that stores information you copy or cut.

Close button In a Windows title bar, the rightmost button; closes the open window, app, and/or document.

Cloud storage File storage locations on the World Wide Web, such as Windows SkyDrive or Dropbox.

Command An instruction to perform a task, such as opening a file or emptying the Recycle Bin.

Command button A button you click to issue instructions to modify applicaton program (app) objects.

Copy To make a duplicate copy of a file, folder, or other object that you want to store in another location.

Default In an app window or dialog box, a value that is automatically set; you can change the default to any valid value.

Desktop apps Application programs (apps), such as Microsoft Office, that open in resizeable windows that you can move and resize to view alongside other app windows; also called traditional apps.

Device A hardware component that is part of your computer system, such as a disk drive, a pointing device, or a touch screen device.

Dialog box A window with controls that lets you tell Windows how you want to complete an application program's (app's) command.

Document window The portion of a application program's (app's) window in which you create the document; displays all or part of an open document.

Double-click To quickly press and release or click the left button on the pointing device twice.

Drag To point to an object, press and hold the left button on the pointing device, move the object to a new location, and then release the left button.

Drag and drop To use a pointing device to move or copy a file or folder directly to a new location instead of using the Clipboard.

Drive A physical location on your computer where you can store files.

Drive name A name for a drive that consists of a letter followed by a colon, such as C: for the hard disk drive.

Dropbox A free online storage site that lets you transfer files that can be retrieved by other people you invite. *See also* Cloud storage.

Edit To make changes to a file.

File A collection of information stored on your computer, such as a letter, video, or app.

File Explorer A Windows accessory that allows you to navigate your computer's file hierarchy and manage your files and folders.

File extension A three- or four-letter sequence, preceded by a period, at the end of a filename that identifies the file as a particular type of document; for example, documents in the Rich Text Format have the file extension .rtf.

File hierarchy The tree-like structure of folders and files on your computer.

File list A section of a window that shows the contents of the folder or drive currently selected in the Navigation pane.

File management The ability to organize folders and files on your computer.

Filename A unique, descriptive name for a file that identifies the file's content.

Folder An electronic container that helps you organize your computer files, like a cardboard folder on your desk; it can contain subfolders for organizing files into smaller groups.

Folder name A unique, descriptive name for a folder that helps identify the folder's contents.

Forum Electronic gathering place where anyone can add questions and answers on computer issues.

Gesture An action you take with your fingertip directly on the screen, such as tapping or swiping, to make a selection or perform a task.

Group In a Microsoft app window's Ribbon, a section containing related command buttons.

Hard disk A built-in, high-capacity, high-speed storage medium for all the software, folders, and files on a computer. Also called a hard drive.

Highlighted Describes the changed appearance of an item or other object, usually a change in its color, background color, and/or border; often used for an object on which you will perform an action, such as a desktop icon.

Icon A small image that represents an item, such as the Recycle Bin on your computer; you can rearrange, add, and delete desktop icons.

Inactive window An open window you are not currently using; if multiple windows are open, the window(s) with the dimmed title bar.

Insertion point In a document or filename, a blinking, vertical bar that indicates where the next character you type will appear.

Keyword A descriptive word or phrase you enter to obtain a list of results that include that word or phrase.

Layout An arrangement of files or folders in a window, such as Large icons or Details. There are eight layouts available.

Library A window that shows files and folders stored in different storage locations; default libraries in Windows 8 include the Documents, Music, Pictures, and Videos libraries.

Link Text or an image that you click to display another location, such as a Help topic, a Web site, or a device.

List box A box that displays a list of options from which you can choose (you may need to scroll and adjust your view to see additional options in the list).

Live tile Updated, "live" content that appears on some apps' tiles on the Windows Start screen, including the Weather app and the News app.

Load To copy and place an app into your computer's memory in preparation for use.

Lock screen The screen that appears when you first start your computer, or after you leave it unattended for a period of time, before the sign-in screen.

Log in To select a user account name when a computer starts up, giving access to that user's files. Also called sign in.

Maximize button On the right side of a window's title bar, the center button of three buttons; used to expand a window so that it fills the entire screen. In a maximized window, this button changes to a Restore button.

Maximized window A window that fills the desktop.

Menu A list of related commands.

Microsoft Community Website A Microsoft Help feature that lets you search forums (electronic gathering places where anyone can add questions and answers on computer issues), Microsoft help files, and even on-screen video demonstrations about selected topics. (Formerly the Microsoft Answers website.)

Microsoft SkyDrive A Microsoft Web site where you can obtain free file storage space, using your own account, that you can share with others; you can access SkyDrive from a laptop, tablet computer, or smartphone.

Microsoft Windows 8 An operating system.

Minimize button On the right side of a window's title bar, the leftmost button of three buttons; use to reduce a window so that it only appears as an icon on the taskbar.

Minimized window A window that is visible only as an icon on the taskbar.

Mouse pointer A small arrow or other symbol on the screen that you move by manipulating the pointing device; also called a pointer.

Move To change the location of a file, folder, or other object by physically placing it in another location.

My Documents folder The folder on your hard drive used to store most of the files you create or receive from others; might contain subfolders to organize the files into smaller groups.

Navigate down To move to a lower level in your computer's file hierarchy.

Navigate up To move to a higher level in your computer's file hierarchy.

Navigation pane A pane in a window that contains links to folders and libraries; click an item in the Navigation pane to display its contents in the file list or click the ◢ or ▷ symbols to display or hide subfolders in the Navigation pane.

Notification area An area on the right side of the Windows 8 taskbar that displays the current time as well as icons representing apps; displays pop-up messages when a program on your computer needs your attention.

Operating system A program that manages the complete operation of your computer and lets you interact with it.

Option button A small circle in a dialog box that you click to select only one of two or more related options.

Pane A section of a window, such as the Navigation pane.

Password A special sequence of numbers and letters that users can use to control who can access the files in their user account area; keeping the password private helps keep users' computer information secure.

Paste To place a copied item from the Clipboard to a location in a document.

Path An address that describes the exact location of a file in a file hierarchy; shows the folder with the highest hierarchy level on the left and steps through each hierarchy level toward the right. Locations are separated by small triangles or by backslashes.

Photos app A Windows 8 app that lets you view and organize your pictures.

Point To position the tip of the mouse pointer over an object, option, or item.

Pointer *See* Mouse pointer.

Pointing device A device that lets you interact with your computer by controlling the movement of the mouse pointer on your computer screen; examples include a mouse, trackball, touchpad, pointing stick, on-screen touch pointer, or a tablet.

Pointing device action A movement you execute with your computer's pointing device to communicate with the computer; the five basic pointing device actions are point, click, double-click, drag, and right-click.

Power button The physical button on your computer that turns your computer on.

Preview pane A pane on the right side of a window that shows the actual contents of a selected file without opening an app; might not work for some types of files.

Program A set of instructions written for a computer, such as an operating system program or an application program; also called an application or an app.

Quick Access toolbar A small toolbar on the left side of a Microsoft application program window's title bar, containing icons that you click to quickly perform common actions, such as saving a file.

RAM (Random Access Memory) The storage location that is part of every computer, that temporarily stores open apps and document data while a computer is on.

Recycle Bin A desktop object that stores folders and files you delete from your hard drive(s) and enables you to restore them.

Removable storage Storage media that you can easily transfer from one computer to another, such as DVDs, CDs, or USB flash drives.

Restore Down button On the right side of a maximized window's title bar, the center of three buttons; use to reduce a window to its last non-maximized size. In a restored window, this button changes to a Maximize button.

Ribbon In many Microsoft app windows, a horizontal strip near the top of the window that contains tabs (pages) of grouped command buttons that you click to interact with the app.

Rich Text Format (RTF) The file format that the WordPad app uses to save files.

Right-click To press and release the right button on the pointing device; use to display a shortcut menu with commands you issue by left-clicking them.

RTF *See* Rich Text Format.

ScreenTip A small box containing informative text that appears when you position the mouse over an object; identifies the object when you point to it.

Scroll To adjust your view to see portions of the app window that are not currently in a window.

Scroll arrow A button at each end of a scroll bar for adjusting your view in a window in small increments in that direction.

Scroll bar A vertical or horizontal bar that appears along the right or bottom side of a window when there is more content than can be displayed within the window, so that you can adjust your view.

Scroll box A box in a scroll bar that you can drag to display a different part of a window.

Search criteria Descriptive text that helps identify the application program (app), folder, file, or Web site you want to locate when conducting a search.

Search Tools tab A tab that appears in the File Explorer window after you click the Search text box; lets you specify a specific search location, limit your search, repeat previous searches, save searches, and open a folder containing a found file.

Select To change the appearance of an item by clicking, double-clicking, or dragging across it, to indicate that you want to perform an action on it.

Select pointer The mouse pointer shape that looks like a white arrow pointing toward the upper-left corner of the screen.

Shortcut An icon that acts as a link to an app, file, folder, or device that you use frequently.

Shortcut menu A menu of context-appropriate commands for an object that opens when you right-click that object.

Shut down To exit the operating system and turn off your computer.

Sign in To select a user account name when a computer starts up, giving access to that user's files. Also called log in.

Single-click *See* Click.

Snap feature For desktop application programs, the Windows 8 feature that lets you drag a window to the left or right side of the screen, where it "snaps" to fill that half of the screen; also, for Windows 8 apps, the feature that lets you position one of two open apps so it occupies one- or two-thirds of the screen.

Sort Change the order of, such as the order of files or folders in a window, based on criteria such as date, file size, or alphabetical by filename.

Spin box A text box with up and down arrows; you can type a setting in the text box or click the arrows to increase or decrease the setting.

Start screen The screen you see after you sign in to Windows 8; contains controls, such as tiles, that let you interact with the Windows 8 operating system.

Subfolder A folder within another folder.

Tab A page in an application program's Ribbon, or in a dialog box, that contains a group of related commands and settings.

Taskbar The horizontal bar at the bottom of the Windows 8 desktop; displays icons representing apps, folders, and/or files on the left, and the Notification area, containing the date and time and special program messages, on the right.

Tile A shaded rectangle on the Windows 8 Start screen that represents an app. *See also* App and Application program.

Title bar The shaded top border of a window that displays the name of the window, folder, or file and the app name. Darker shading indicates the active window.

Toolbar In an application program, a set of buttons, lists, and menus you can use to issue program commands.

Touch pointer A pointer on the screen for performing pointing operations with a finger if touch input is available on your computer.

Traditional apps Application programs (apps), such as Microsoft Office, that open in windows that you can move and resize to view alongside other app windows; also called desktop apps.

USB flash drive A removable storage device for folders and files that you plug into a USB port on your computer; makes it easy to transport folders and files to other computers. Also called a pen drive, flash drive, jump drive, keychain drive, or thumb drive.

User account A special area in a computer's operating system where users can store their own files and preferences.

User interface The controls that let you interact with an operating system or an application program (app).

View A set of appearance choices for folder contents, such as Large Icons view or Details view.

Window A rectangular-shaped work area that displays an app or a collection of files, folders, and Windows tools.

Window control icons The set of three buttons on the right side of a window's title bar that let you control the window's state, such as minimized, maximized, restored to its previous open size, or closed.

Windows 8 apps Apps (application programs) for Windows 8 that have a single purpose, such as Photos, News, or SkyDrive.

Windows 8 UI The Windows 8 user interface. *See also* User interface.

Windows accessories Application programs (apps), such as Paint or WordPad, that come with the Windows 8 operating system.

Windows desktop An electronic work area that lets you organize and manage your information, much like your own physical desktop.

Windows Search The Windows feature that lets you look for files and folders on your computer storage devices; to search, type text in the Search text box in the title bar of any open window, or click the Office button and type text in the Search programs and files text box.

Windows Website A link in the Windows Help app that lets you find Windows 8 resources such as blogs, video tours, and downloads.

Index